mor
Sex and the

"A groundbreaking call to action."
—Kiera Van Gelder, author of *The Buddha and the Borderline*

"A book well worth reading."
—Steve Hagen, author of *Buddhism Plain and Simple*

"Incisive and compassionate. Highly recommended."
—Brian Victoria, author of *Zen at War*

"By emphasizing the humanness of even the wisest teacher and the importance of transparency, Edelstein provides wise, clear counsel for spiritual teachers, students, and those who care for them that will undoubtedly reduce the risk of problematic relationships, as well as help those who find themselves having crossed boundaries act with kindness and care to extricate themselves from these harmful situations. Students and teachers in other contexts will also benefit from the wisdom in these pages. Edelstein's willingness to look at what is so often hidden with unwavering clarity and compassion is an immense gift to us all."
—Lizabeth Roemer, Ph.D., co-author of *The Mindful Way Through Anxiety*

"Finally, a book that addresses sexual misconduct within spiritual communities with equanimity and smarts. An invaluable book for students and leaders alike."
—Elizabeth Jarrett Andrew, author of *Writing the Sacred Journey*

"At long last, this book offers a clear, objective look at the causes and effects of such behavior. An enlightening must-read for every spiritual student and community governing board."
—Thérèse Jacobs-Stewart, author of *Mindfulness and the 12 Steps*

"A well-thought-out and eminently practical guide."
—Mic Hunter, author of *Honor Betrayed* and *Abused Boys*

"Sexual energies often feed the shadow side of many student/teacher relationships. When ignored or repressed they can distort the relationship, shifting it from liberation to exploitation. Scott Edelstein's masterful book shines light into the shadows, freeing both teacher and student to receive the true gift of spiritual partnership."
—Rabbi Rami Shapiro, author of *The Sacred Art of Lovingkindness*

"Scott Edelstein reminds us that spiritual teachers and students alike are graced with a wonderful, mysterious, and volatile sexual energy. This down-to-earth book is good medicine, helping us all to take care of ourselves, each other, and our spiritual communities."
—Erik Fraser Storlie, author of *Nothing on My Mind*

"This book is thoroughly refreshing and long-overdue! Edelstein strikes a tone that is at once urgent, funny, compassionate, and sex-positive. First and foremost, he encourages spiritual community members to embrace their leaders' humanity while holding them to the highest level of ethical standards. This should be required reading for every student and leader of a spiritual community."
—Marjorie P. Kroeger, founder and clinical director of The Stony Brook Center for the treatment of compulsive sexual behavior and sex addiction

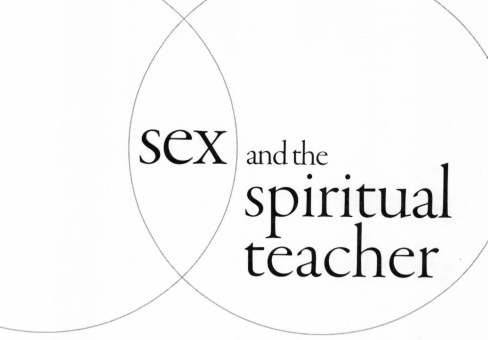

sex and the spiritual teacher

why it happens, when it's a problem, and what we all can do

by Scott Edelstein

Introduction by Mic Hunter • Afterword by Anne Katherine

WISDOM PUBLICATIONS • BOSTON

Wisdom Publications
199 Elm Street
Somerville MA 02144 USA

Library of Congress Cataloging-in-Publication Data
Edelstein, Scott.
 Sex and the spiritual teacher : why it happens, when it's a problem, and what we all can do / by Scott Edelstein ; introduction by Mic Hunter ; afterword by Anne Katherine.
   p. cm.
 Includes bibliographical references (p.   ) and index.
 ISBN 0-86171-596-9 (pbk. : alk. paper)
  1. Sex crimes—Religious aspects. 2. Religious leaders—Sexual behavior. 3. Teacher-student relationships—Religious aspects. I. Title.
 BL65.S42E34 2010
 362.88—dc22

                              2010052128

eBook ISBN: 978-08-6171-6449
ISBN 13: 978-08-6171-5961

15 14 13 12 11
5   4   3   2   1

Designed and typeset by Gopa & Ted2, Inc. Set in Sabon 10.76/15.

Wisdom Publications' books are printed on acid-free paper and meet the guidelines for the permanence and durability of the Committee on Production Guidelines for Book Longevity of the Council on Library Resources.

Printed in the United States of America.

This book was produced with environmental mindfulness. We have elected to print this title on 30% PCW recycled paper. As a result, we have saved the following resources: 20 trees, 6 million BTUs of energy, 1,892 lbs. of greenhouse gases, 9,115 gallons of water, and 553 lbs. of solid waste. For more information, please visit our website, www.wisdompubs.org. This paper is also FSC certified. For more information, please visit www.fscus.org.

Table of Contents

What You Need to Know About This Book

THIS BOOK is about spiritual teachers who have sex with their students, the suffering that such encounters often cause, and what all of us can do about it.

This is not a book of finger-pointing or whistle-blowing. Nor does it defend or apologize for spiritual teachers who lose their way. In fact, as we will see, the more we attack *or* defend wayward teachers, the more we encourage their waywardness.

Instead, this book is intended to create greater safety and spiritual intimacy between spiritual teachers and their students, and among members of spiritual communities.

Everything in this book is eminently practical and down-to-earth. It's about real human emotions, interactions, and dilemmas—and genuine safety and suffering. Almost nothing in it is academic or theoretical. It's written for anyone who is (or hopes to become) part of a spiritual community: students, teachers, clergy, lay leaders, and even casual visitors.

Part I of this book offers practical analysis and action for individuals; Part II offers solutions and strategies for spiritual communities. Although my hope is that a great many spiritual communities will use this book, it's not a mere manual or guidebook. It's a book of inquiry, awareness, and social and spiritual change.

Why Me?

I'm not a psychologist, sociologist, spiritual teacher, or member of the clergy. Why, then, do I dare to write this book, and why do my words deserve your attention?

First, I'm a longtime writer and speaker whose work often focuses on spiritual subjects. In fact, this book grew from a talk I gave in 2004 at Dharma Field Zen Center in Minneapolis.

Second, I've been a member of several spiritual communities for more than two decades; I've had the good fortune to know many spiritual teachers as friends and acquaintances; and I've served as editor and literary agent for two such teachers. I've shared homes with two spiritual teachers, and served as confidant, sounding board, and career counselor for both. I've spent countless hours with spiritual teachers during their off-duty hours—in restaurants, bars, and their own living rooms. I've watched as several of my friends made the transition from students to spiritual teachers. Over the past thirty-five years, I've studied with several spiritual · teachers—most of them in the Zen tradition, some of them well known. I've also attended retreats and workshops led by other spiritual teachers from many traditions (though mostly Buddhist and Jewish). And I went through my own distress and disappointment as I learned that some of the teachers I knew and respected had had sex with their students.

Though this background qualifies me to write this book, I don't claim to have arrived at perfect or definitive answers—or at anything that might be called enlightenment. Although I stand behind everything in this volume, I am very open to discussion, debate, and—in cases where I've erred—correction. You'll find an ongoing discussion of the topics in this book on my websites, thespiritualteachersite.com and sexandthespiritualteacher.com.

A Few Words About Words

Religious and spiritual terms are notoriously tough—and often impossible—to standardize. We can, however, settle on some specific definitions within particular contexts. Here, then, is a quick look at some terms I'll use throughout this book, and their definitions:

Spiritual teacher. This term refers to anyone who works closely and one-to-one with others to help them explore life's most important questions, live wholeheartedly, and find their spiritual way in the world. The term thus includes spiritual directors, coaches, and counselors.

 The relationship between spiritual teachers and each of their students is, by nature, quite intimate. It is thus qualitatively different from most clergy/congregant relationships, in which clergy serve primarily as groups' spiritual and ceremonial leaders.

 The great majority of spiritual teachers, as I define them, are ordained priests, ministers, monks, nuns, rabbis, imams, etc. Some, however, have no formal credentials. Most serve as the spiritual leaders of congregations, sanghas, or other formal groups, but some are itinerant, going from group to group and city to city. Others work entirely (or primarily) on a one-to-one basis with students, who may live all over the region, country, or world.

 Many spiritual communities have more than one teacher. Throughout this book, when I refer to a hypothetical spiritual community's "teacher," please read this as "teacher or teachers."

Student. I use this word as a catch-all term that also means follower, disciple, protégé, mentee, etc.

Spiritual community. I use this term broadly. It can be a congregation; a class or study group; residents of a monastery, religious center, or ashram; some other cohort (e.g., participants in a retreat); or all the people who consider themselves students of the same teacher.

The Absolute. Throughout this book I use this term as a generic stand-in for God, the Divine, the Whole, the One, the Unconditioned, the Unborn, *ein sof*, *Brahman*, the ground of being, enlightenment, etc. Whenever you see the Absolute, substitute whatever term you prefer that expresses the Inexpressible One.

Monogamy. Although this word has many definitions, in this book it refers to a loving, committed relationship with one—and only one—other human being. This includes but is not limited to marriage.

He, she, they. There's no ideal pronoun for referring to a hypothetical spiritual teacher. Some choices are cumbersome, some sexist, some grating, some inane. Since all options fall short, I've opted for "they," "them," or "their" in most cases—e.g., "A spiritual teacher can benefit enormously from having a teacher of their own." However, when I write of a hypothetical teacher who has sexually transgressed—or been accused of transgressing—I've used a masculine pronoun, simply because (as we shall see later) the great majority of such transgressors are male. This strategy, while imperfect, seems most reader friendly.

An Invitation

If you're part of a spiritual community—or hope to become part of one some day—this book is for and about you. It also asks something deeply important of you: that you do more than merely read and digest my words.

I invite you to use this book to make spiritual life safer and more intimate for all of us—one person, relationship, and community at a time.

Sex, Spirit, and Safety

by Mic Hunter

THROUGHOUT HISTORY, people have commented on the close association between sexuality and spirituality. Psychotherapist Carl Jung noted that when his patients brought sexual questions to him, they invariably turned out to be questions concerning spirituality—and vice versa.

Perhaps this is because sexuality and spirituality are two of the most personal—and most significant—aspects of what it means to be human. Our sexuality begins even before birth: advanced imaging devices show that males in the womb get erections. Many parents can attest to the fact that babies of both sexes take delight in playing with their genitals. And two of the first categories into which toddlers learn to place people are "boy" and "girl."

Shortly after youngsters develop a sense of sexuality, many start to ponder spirituality. Children as young as three begin to ask questions about God, even if they are raised in homes that are not religious.

As children grow older, the association between spirituality and sexuality becomes ever more entwined, as authority figures instruct them to look to religious traditions in order to determine which sexual behaviors and thoughts are acceptable and which ones are discouraged, forbidden, or considered sinful.

The significant roles that both sexuality and spirituality play in our lives make interpersonal boundaries necessary. The term *boundaries* can sometimes sound like nothing more than psychobabble spewed on daytime talk shows—but any individual, organization, or community that ignores the importance of boundaries is headed for serious trouble.

Interpersonal boundaries are not the creation of modern-day psychologists or business consultants; they have existed for as long as humans have lived in groups. The age-old taboo against incest exists in part because our ancestors realized long ago that sex between parents and children is, among other things, one of the most psychologically damaging boundary violations. A similar dynamic exists between mental health professionals and their clients; as a result, professional organizations consider sex between clinicians and their clients to be unethical, and state governments have declared it illegal.

Likewise, extensive (and often painful) experience has shown that when sex occurs between a spiritual guide and a student, the teacher-student relationship is often damaged, sometimes irrevocably. In some cases, the student's own sense of spirituality is similarly broken.

Any relationship potent enough to promote growth and healing is also powerful enough to harm. This is especially so with the relationship that exists between a spiritual teacher and a student hungry for spiritual knowledge and growth.

Until now, this vital topic has not been properly addressed. Fortunately, with the publication of *Sex and the Spiritual Teacher*, we now have a well-thought-out and eminently practical guide to protecting the integrity of students, teachers, and the organizations to which they belong.

Now, more than ever, the world needs the healing power that comes with healthy spirituality. Every loving act makes more loving acts likely. This book is such an act.

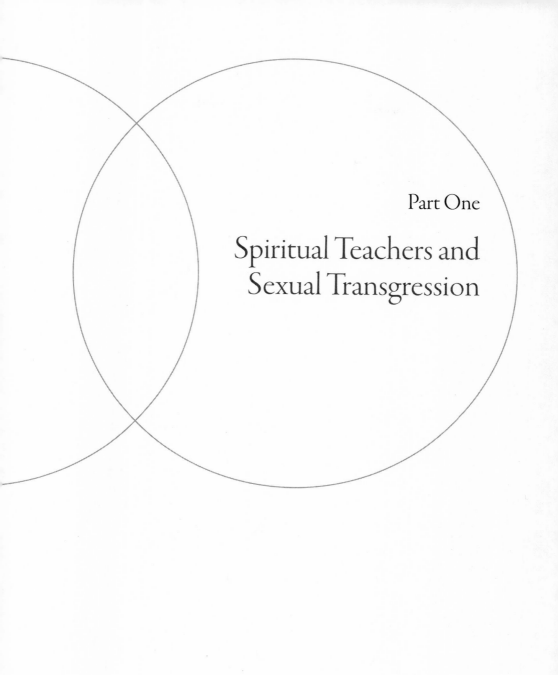

Part One

Spiritual Teachers and Sexual Transgression

Chapter 1

Five Narrow Views

OUR SATURDAY MORNING meditation group usually starts with hugs, smiles, and jokes. But today it begins with Sarah's tears.

Sarah is the group's matriarch. She speaks four languages, has lived in four countries, and survived multiple wars. The rest of us often ask her spiritual questions, and she often gives wonderfully clear, yet deeply mystical answers. She laughs easily, often at her own mistakes.

Yet as we take our seats on this gorgeous spring morning, Sarah suddenly begins to weep.

I touch her arm and offer her a tissue. "What's wrong?"

She dabs at her eyes for some time before she is able to talk. Eventually she mentions the name of a well-known spiritual teacher. "I was his student; he was my guru, my *rebbe*. For years I felt a special connection with him. He was always so wise, so mesmerizing, so inspiring. When I was in the room with him, I felt something shift and deepen inside me. Wherever he went, he packed the house." She takes a long, sobbing breath. "Yesterday I found out he sexually abused women. Dozens of women, many of them his students. Some of them young girls. For over twenty-five years. *Twenty-five years*. He just admitted to all of it." She shakes her head and blows her nose noisily.

I start to speak, but she touches my hand and shakes her head. She needs to say more.

"I don't understand how he could be so wise and inspiring, yet so abusive."

Sexual Misconduct: A Long and Thriving Tradition

Sadly, Sarah's spiritual teacher was anything but unique. The problem of spiritual teachers seducing or sexually abusing their students tarnishes every spiritual tradition, in seemingly every culture—and recorded cases go back many hundreds of years. These misdeeds damage the lives of women and men, children and adults, the rich and the poor, the foolish and the wise, the gullible and the discerning.

A list of spiritual teachers who have committed sexual transgressions during the past few decades reads almost like a Who's Who of modern spiritual figures, and includes priests, ministers, rabbis, gurus, yogis, roshis, senseis, swamis, lamas, maggids, and imams. Sometimes their misconduct involves other transgressions as well (misappropriation of money, physical or emotional abuse, attempted brainwashing, etc.). This widespread misconduct has created scandal after scandal for these teachers, and much suffering for their students and spiritual communities.

With very few exceptions, each of these teachers is or was male;* each offered something genuinely worthwhile to their students; each knew that sex with their students could have potentially damaging consequences for those students; and each—including those teachers raised in other cultures—understood that the prevailing social

---

* I do not mean to suggest that female spiritual teachers don't commit sexual misdeeds. Some do. It is also a huge mistake to think that female spiritual teachers do not routinely struggle with the temptation to have sex with their students. Still, it does appear that sexual misconduct is far more common among male spiritual teachers.

In multiple studies by Kenneth Pope, Jacqueline Bouhoutsos, and Peter Rutter, 96% of helping professionals who had sex with their clients, patients, or students were male. Some prominent psychologists believe this asymmetry may be at least somewhat exaggerated, in much the same way that early studies of sexual abuse by Catholic priests "revealed" that few of their victims were male. Nevertheless, even if the actual number of female teachers who had sex with their students were five times higher than studies show, they would still make up only 24% of the total.

norms prohibited such sexual relationships. Many of these teachers were married, and thus had vows of fidelity to uphold, as well as (presumably) willing sexual partners. Some had taken vows of celibacy. So why did they act against the best interests of their students, their own spiritual communities, and, ultimately, themselves?

There are five commonly accepted answers to this question. They are deeply divergent, and in some cases mutually exclusive:

1. These transgressions are rare exceptions—the outcomes of a few troubled teachers' psychological problems.
2. Men are pigs. Whether they're spiritual teachers, college professors, or plumbers, men just can't keep their pants zipped up.
3. Spiritual teachers are all frauds who delude others, themselves, or both.
4. The misconduct is not about sex, but power. The spiritual teachers are power junkies, and sex is simply a means of exercising their power.
5. The previous four positions are all bogus. The teacher and the student are both consenting adults who are responsible for their own actions. These so-called transgressions are legitimate, consensual relationships.

In this book I argue that *all five* of these explanations are largely off the mark. In part this is because each one lumps all sexual transgressions together, as if they were variations on a single consistent theme (which they are not); in part it is because they assume that all transgressing teachers share a single personality profile (which, of course, they don't).

In fact, as we look closely, we will see that there are three distinct types of spiritual teachers who lose their way: *exploiters*, *errants*, and *exceptionalists*. In Chapter 2, I'll look at and define each of these groups; I'll also discuss the common variations within each group.

Similarly, the catch-all term "sexual misconduct" covers a very wide range of transgressions, from felonies to exploitation to poor judgment. These include (from most to least harmful) sexual assault; role bait-and-switch; sex as a spiritual teaching or tool;

power plays; sex as a prize or honor; verbal manipulation; inauthentic professions of love and/or proposals of marriage; sexual dealmaking; ordinary seduction (or attempted seduction); simple, straightforward offers of sex; and giving in to mutual attraction.

Teachers who transgress in any of the first ten ways are unlikely to maintain long-term monogamy or celibacy, and should not normally be permitted to continue as teachers. However, for some teachers who give in to mutual attraction, and do so only once, there is considerable hope.

Furthermore, there is much that we can do—as individuals, spiritual communities, and a society—to help prevent our spiritual teachers from losing their way. The last nine chapters of this book offer a wide array of these practical preventive measures.

Sexual Transgression by the Numbers

The web brims with sites that report the sexual misdeeds of spiritual teachers. Some focus on a single tradition; others report on the misconduct of spiritual teachers from a variety of traditions (as well as those outside of mainstream traditions).*

No one has recently conducted a survey to determine what percentage of spiritual teachers have had sex with their students. In 1985, however, insight meditation teacher and writer Jack Kornfield published a survey of 54 spiritual teachers from several non-Western traditions. Kornfield asked these 48 men and 6 women† two questions:

1. Are you celibate? and
2. Have you had a sexual relationship with at least one of your students?

---

* One site, theawarenesscenter.org, for example, blows the whistle on exploitive Jewish spiritual teachers, while guruphiliac.blogspot.com follows a wide range of exploitive spiritual teachers.

† In 1985, far fewer women were trained (or permitted) to become spiritual teachers—hence the imbalance in Kornfield's sample.

The results: 87% of those teachers who were not celibate—34 out of 39—admitted to having had at least one such relationship. If we include the celibate teachers in our sample as well, then 63% of all teachers surveyed had had sex with at least one of their students.

Kornfield's survey is small and decades old, and it neglects teachers in the Abrahamic traditions, as well as well-known mavericks who don't strongly identify with any one tradition. Yet it should nevertheless give us pause. After all, how would you feel if you learned that 63% of doctors had had sex with their patients, or 63% of professors had had sex with their students, or 63% of psychologists had had sex with their clients?*

Since 1985, not a single follow-up survey has been conducted on spiritual teachers' sexual involvement with their students. Arguably, this is itself something of a scandal. However, more recent anecdotal evidence—i.e., an ongoing stream of new scandals—suggests that widespread sexual misconduct continues, though almost certainly at a rate lower than 63%. In any case, it does seem fair to say that, among all helping professionals, spiritual teachers have earned the #1 spot for sexual transgression.

In fact, as this book will show, the prevalence of such misdeeds is not the result of *any* of the five standard positions described earlier. Rather, it reflects a welter of interrelated causes—some of them quite surprising:

▶ The singular intimacy between spiritual teachers and their students—an intimacy that spans all traditions.

▶ The psychology of masculine sexuality—in particular, the ability to be wise, compassionate, loving, aware, and careful

---

* Multiple studies show that, in fact, roughly 10–20% (depending on the profession) of male professionals in these fields have had sex with their clients, patients, or students, and that 30% of clergy have been sexual with their congregants. These figures are themselves high enough to cause Peter Rutter to declare, in *Sex in the Forbidden Zone*, that "sexual exploitation of professional relationships is epidemic in our society." It may be epidemic in other cultures as well, but to my knowledge no one has sufficiently studied the phenomenon elsewhere.

in most areas of life, yet foolish, acquisitive, or predatory
when it comes to sex.

▶ The unique mega-alpha status of spiritual teachers in most
spiritual communities.

▶ The arrogance that often springs from genuine but limited
spiritual insight.

▶ The counterintuitive reality that the folks who sexually transgress tend to be well known and well trained.

▶ The exceptionally large power differential between spiritual
teachers and their students—a differential much larger than
the one between ordinary spiritual leaders and their congregants, or college professors and their students.

▶ Spiritual communities' failure to sufficiently encourage (and
require) conscientious behavior from their teachers—and
their unintentional support of misconduct.

▶ The unacknowledged sexual power of spiritual teachers' students, and the ways in which they wield it.

▶ The many expected and unexpected ways in which celibacy
encourages sexual misconduct.

None of these causes takes spiritual teachers off the hook, of
course. Nor does any qualify as an acceptable excuse for misconduct. However, the closer we scrutinize these causes, the more
deeply we understand them—and the wiser we become about supporting our spiritual teachers' wholesome actions.

Focusing on Sanity and Safety

This is not a book of blame. My primary concerns are for the safety
of women and men who walk a spiritual path, and with the health
of the spiritual communities to which they belong.

Nor is this a compendium of spiritual teachers' misdeeds.* Other

---

* One such compendium is Geoffrey D. Falk's book *Stripping the Gurus: Sex, Violence,
Abuse and Enlightenment*, which is available as both a print volume and a free e-book.

writers have done a good job of revealing and cataloguing many spiritual teachers' past transgressions, so there's no need for me to do it again here.

The purposes of my own book are more constructive. First, it examines the mental and emotional lives of spiritual teachers who have sex with their students, as well as those of teachers who stay lovingly monogamous or honorably celibate. It looks at the complex of forces that tempt otherwise insightful, compassionate, and well-intentioned teachers to lose their way—and that tempt some of their students to lose their own way as well. It investigates a variety of practices that can become breeding grounds for sexual misconduct, including celibacy, guru-disciple relationships, sex as a spiritual teaching, and "crazy wisdom"—i.e., spiritual guidance or insight expressed in a bizarre or seemingly nonsensical form. It analyzes why most of our current efforts to keep spiritual teachers from transgressing usually don't (and, in fact, can't) work. Perhaps most importantly, however, it suggests a set of practices and structures that can build community, encourage healthy student-teacher relationships, increase trust and intimacy between teachers and their students, and help authentic spiritual teachers stay happily monogamous or celibate.

None of this requires miracles or profound mystical experience. Almost all of it is readily doable with the people and institutions already in place. Furthermore, nearly all of it can be done reasonably quickly and without enormous effort, expense, or gnashing of teeth. This book lays out and knits together the necessary pieces— and, I hope, provides the inspiration for us to get moving in the right direction.

Yet spiritual teachers are not the people who must take the

Falk's detailed, snarky, meticulously-researched book covers dozens of well-known spiritual teachers from a wide range of traditions, as well as many from outside of those traditions. His book is an eye-opening read and provides many valuable cautionary tales. You can also, of course, access many hundreds of tales of misconduct simply by Googling "spiritual teacher" and "scandal."

all-important first step. That responsibility falls to us: their students, followers, disciples, and protégés.

That first step is this: *We must be willing to let go of whom we wish, hope, and desire our spiritual teachers to be, and begin to relate to them as they actually are.* This means fully accepting—in our hearts, minds, and guts—some painful but essential truths:

All spiritual teachers—no matter how enlightened (or deluded)—are human beings, with the same physical, mental, and emotional equipment as the rest of us. Indeed, if they weren't, how could we possibly follow in their footsteps and what could they really teach us? When we accept that our teachers are fundamentally just like us, we give ourselves a huge gift: we accept *in ourselves* the potential to embody the same wisdom, compassion, and spirit of service that we value in them.

All spiritual teachers—no matter how enlightened—make some mistakes and misjudgments. From the viewpoint of the Absolute, we can say that there are no accidents, or that the very concept of "mistake" is a mental construct. Fair enough. But on the relative level—the level on which it's true to say, "Look both ways before crossing the street or you might get run over"—spiritual teachers can and do err.

Spiritual teachers are susceptible to temptation, sexual and otherwise. Many can resist it far better, and for far longer, than most of us—and many are able to see it coming well in advance. But spiritual teachers are also exposed to far greater—and far more frequent—temptations than most of us.

Many spiritual teachers are sexy. Some are extremely sexy. The same is true of some of their students. This is an essential—if obvious—part of the mix, yet few discussions of the topic acknowledge it.

It is entirely possible for a spiritual teacher to be wise, compassionate, empathetic, and inspiring, and at the same time sexually exploitive. This may seem entirely contradictory, but spiritual teachers have proven it true time after time. For better or worse, we humans are often contradictory creatures—especially when it comes to sex, power, and vocation.

If these points all seem obvious to you, then congratulations; please read on. As you will see, there is much that you can do to make the world safer for our sisters and brothers with spiritual inclinations.

If you disagree with any of the above statements, or believe that your own teacher is infallible, or more than human, or incapable of doing harm or creating karma, please read on anyway. (And if and when your teacher becomes embroiled in a scandal, I hope you'll take a second look at this book.)

Why It Matters

Any honest discussion of spiritual teachers' sexual misconduct must begin by addressing two basic questions:

1. Why is sex between spiritual teachers and their students so problematic?, and
2. How does the issue of sexual misconduct by spiritual teachers differ from that of sexual misconduct by ordinary clergy (e.g., the parish priest, the minister of the corner church, or the rabbi of the synagogue down the block)?

At the heart of every healthy student-teacher relationship are four essential elements:

1. The student's desire to become wiser or more fully human
2. The teacher's overt or implied commitment to assist the student in that endeavor
3. The teacher's parallel commitment to consistently act in the student's best interests
4. The student's faith that the teacher will honor these commitments

At the heart of most *unhealthy* student-teacher relationships is the teacher's failure to honor one or more of these commitments. In healthy relationships, the student develops a deep and abiding trust in the teacher, and this trust is rewarded. In unhealthy ones it is violated.

There is both great spiritual intimacy and an enormous power differential in relationships between spiritual teachers and their students. As this intimacy increases—with sustained contact, or during spiritual retreats, or when the teacher meets with the student one-to-one—this power differential increases as well.

When a spiritual teacher uses this power wisely and skillfully, the student is encouraged to wake up, grow up, and open up. But when a teacher uses the student for his own gratification, sexual or otherwise, the student feels smaller and less fully human. With rare exceptions,* this is so even when the sexual attraction is very much mutual, the sex is mutually initiated (or initiated by the student), and both people find the sex thrilling and delightful. Ultimately, over time, the student feels betrayed or punished for their whole-heartedness, intimacy, trust, and spiritual aspiration. Usually, their faith and trust in the teacher are broken. Often they become less able to trust other spiritual teachers or leaders. In some cases, they may also struggle to trust their spiritual tradition, or all traditions, or potential romantic partners. Their trust in *themselves* may be damaged as well. They may think, *Look what I got myself into. I don't know how to choose a teacher. And look how far astray I went. I have no ability to follow a spiritual path. Maybe I should just give up on this spiritual stuff.*

Typically, this betrayal is not limited to the individual student, but is felt throughout the entire spiritual community. Though the misconduct may have been very specific, it tends to create a ripple effect that does wide-ranging and long-term damage.

To get a sense of this, imagine for a moment that you have agreed to open-heart surgery to repair a faulty heart valve. You trust the surgeon, who seems like a compassionate and capable man who will practice his art as well as he can, and who will act in your best interests at all times.

Now imagine that when you awaken from your surgery, you see

---

* Please note both parts of this phrase: yes, there are exceptions—and they are quite rare.

your longtime partner and two of your siblings standing nearby, all in tears. "Am I dying?" you ask. Your partner takes your hand and says grimly, "No. Your valve's fine. But while you were under the anesthetic, the surgeon had sex with you—twice."

Now ask yourself how much you will trust surgeons, and medical professionals in general, over the next few months. Then consider how much your partner and your family will trust these professionals in the future.

Similar damage can be done when a spiritual teacher asks or encourages a student to have sex with him—even if the student says no and the teacher immediately backs off. In attempting to change his role from teacher to lover—or from teacher to lover *and* teacher—he violates a personal boundary. For some students, this may be no big deal; the old boundaries and relationship can be quickly restored, and little or no harm is done. But others may feel that, simply by making the overture, the spiritual teacher has violated a near-sacred trust.

Let's return to the example of our wayward heart surgeon for a moment. Imagine that you're near the end of your first meeting with him, and he concludes by saying, "You're all set. You're scheduled for surgery for Tuesday morning. Here's a booklet that will outline what you can expect after the surgery, and how you can most quickly heal. Before you go, though—I think you are totally hot. Want to do it on the examining table?"

We students expect our spiritual teachers to always act in our best interests, and to put those interests before their own gratification. Unsurprisingly, then, when teachers fail to fulfill this expectation, we naturally trust them less, and become less willing to be honest and vulnerable in their presence.

Spiritual Teachers vs. Ordinary Clergy

Now let's look at the second question: How are the ethical issues surrounding spiritual teachers' sexual misdeeds different from those of sexual misconduct by ordinary clergy?

There are two essential distinctions here. First, for spiritual teachers, the temptations to transgress are far stronger and more varied. (We'll explore the nature of these temptations in later chapters.) Second, when spiritual teachers do lose their way, the emotional wounds they can inflict are potentially far greater. Once again the reasons for this are the especially large power differential between teacher and student, the great personal trust typically invested by students in their teachers, and the spiritual and emotional intimacy that arises in such relationships.

Furthermore, in a teacher-student relationship, the student usually chooses the teacher not because of the teacher's institutional role, but because of the energy, compassion, openness, and/or spiritual wisdom that the student sees (or believes) that the teacher possesses. The student thus expects a great deal *more* from a spiritual teacher than the mere fulfillment of a religious role. In this way the teacher-student relationship closely mirrors that of therapist and client. Any boundary violation by a spiritual teacher is therefore felt especially deeply, and often does great emotional damage.

Compare this with the relationships between most spiritual leaders and their congregants. Typically, these clergy marry and bury, lead services and rituals, and sometimes counsel individuals, couples, and families. Most of their congregants see them primarily in roles that are institutional and ceremonial rather than personal. In most cases, too, these clergy provide little or no one-to-one spiritual guidance to their congregants. While their relationships with congregants tend to be warm, they are rarely spiritually intimate. Furthermore, when such a spiritual leader leaves one congregation to lead another, most congregants stay with their community rather than follow the cleric to their new institutional home.

This distinction between spiritual teacher and common clergy is not about formal title, since many clergy in all religious traditions are also spiritual teachers, and vice versa. Rather, it is about the essential nature of the relationship.

This book does *not* look at ordinary clergy who sexually lose their way—not because such investigations aren't necessary, but because many excellent ones have already been published.* Two other distinctions are worth noting here. As we will see in the next chapter, we students often let spiritual teachers get away with behavior we would never accept from ordinary clergy, let alone from our doctors, professors, piano-tuners, or dry cleaners. All too often, we also accept outrageous excuses from wayward spiritual teachers for their behavior—excuses that we would find laughably lame coming from anyone else.

A Notable Exception

In theory, it is possible for a wise and compassionate teacher and an emotionally healthy student to fall deeply in love with each other; to manage, from the beginning of the relationship, to be equal partners in love while maintaining a healthy teacher-student relationship; and to live more or less happily in this way for the rest of their lives.

In practice, however, such an arrangement appears to be all but impossible.† I would bet against it every time, though I stop just short of suggesting that it has never occurred and never can.

---

*There are dozens of useful and eye-opening books on this subject. Some of the best include *Understanding Clergy Misconduct in Religious Systems* by Candace R. Benyei; *Sex, Priests, and Secret Codes* by Thomas P. Doyle, A. W. Richard Sipe, and Patrick J. Wall; *Responding to Clergy Misconduct* by FaithTrust Institute; *Is Nothing Sacred?* by Marie Fortune; *Sexual Abuse by Clergy* by Marie Fortune and James N. Poling; *When a Congregation Is Betrayed* edited by Beth Ann Gaede; *Questions and Answers About Clergy Sexual Misconduct* by Elisabeth A. Horst; *Restoring the Soul of a Church* edited by Nancy Myer Hopkins and Mark Laaser; *Preventing Sexual Abuse in Congregations* by Karen A. McClintock; *Bless Me Father for I Have Sinned* edited by Thomas G. Plante; *Sin Against the Innocents* edited by Thomas G. Plante; *Sacrilege* by Leon J. Podles; *Wolves Within the Fold* edited by Anson Shupe; *Bad Pastors* edited by Anson Shupe, William A. Stacey, and Susan E. Darnell; and *Sex, Priests, and Power* by A. W. Richard Sipe.

† Some mental health professionals believe that a healthy sexual relationship between a spiritual teacher and their student is *ipso facto* impossible—and that such a relationship is thus, by definition, never consensual. Others, such as Mic Hunter, stop just short of making such black-and-white pronouncements. I stand with Hunter on this, in part because such unequivocal statements create their own problems, in part because they proscribe the very relationships I describe (and approve of) on the following page.

Nevertheless, because the odds against its success are so steep—and the likelihood of at least one person coming to emotional harm are so strong—many spiritual communities wisely forbid it.

What *is* possible, and not terribly uncommon, is a loving partnership that forms between two mindful and loving adults, one of whom *later* becomes the other's spiritual teacher. This can be entirely wholesome, because there is no inherent power differential or role confusion; when the student-teacher relationship develops later on, it does not replace the loving romantic partnership, but is instead developed beside or astride it, at least in the best such cases.

These relationships can evolve in two ways. In some cases, one member of a couple starts out as student or disciple or "ordinary" cleric, and, over time, moves into a teaching role, after which their partner signs on as their student. In others, a spiritual teacher meets, courts, and becomes the partner of someone who has a different teacher, or no teacher at all; over time, after a loving, equal relationship has been established, the partner becomes their student as well.

Indeed, it is often a pleasure to be in the presence of such couples, especially those who have been together for many years, because the spiritual teacher is usually cut absolutely no domestic slack. ("Sugar Pie, I don't *care* if you were up all night planning a week-long retreat; that was your choice, and it's still your turn to do the dishes.") Also, the teacher's partner knows every one of their warts, weaknesses, and limitations, and thus helps them stay humble. ("Hon, you know what would make me really happy right now? If you put the toolbox away and called the appliance-repair people. Remember what happened when you tried to repair the lawn mower?")

Such dual-role relationships are not easy to maintain, and they require a great deal of love, patience, respect, and skill. But they can and do sometimes work, and when they do they are often models of loving conduct.

What Does It Mean to Be a Student?

It's also important to acknowledge that what I call a student-teacher relationship can differ dramatically from tradition to tradition, from teacher to teacher, and even from student to student.

Often two people will formally declare their teacher-student relationship in a ceremony, or via an exchange of letters or emails, or in a conversation. In these cases, each person makes a commitment to the other, and in the process creates a strong spiritual bond and a good deal of spiritual intimacy. Students in these relationships can be deeply harmed if their teachers break the boundaries of those relationships—and the stronger the bond, the more potential damage can be done.

However, not every student-teacher relationship is formally declared or spiritually intimate. Near the other end of the continuum of intimacy are those student-teacher relationships that are much more informal and much less clearly defined. There may be no vows, no formal or implicit agreement, and no commitments made by one person to the other.

At the far end of this continuum are "relationships" that may not qualify as relationships at all. If you occasionally attend talks by Sister Joan Chittister, are you her student or not? What if you also read her books? If you take part in a retreat led by Sufi teacher Kabir Helminski and you stay interested in him and his work, does that make you his student?

Consider the example of a writer and speaker I know. Although he is formally authorized as a Zen teacher, he doesn't accept students at all. In fact, as of this writing, he doesn't call himself a spiritual teacher, and encourages people not to think of him as such.

For several years, this fellow led meditation and discussions on Saturday mornings, as well as half-day retreats every month or two, at an ecumenical center in California. He answered questions, but otherwise didn't work one-to-one with people. He says, "Anyone who wanted to come was welcome. Did that make them my students? When someone asks to formally become my student, I say no." As with most things in life, there are (and always will be) grey areas here—and during those years this man arguably hung out in Greyville.

The point here is not to figure out where to draw the line, or to try to make Greyville smaller or less grey. Indeed, such efforts inevitably fail—and they're sometimes priggish and intrusive, too. Instead, we simply need to keep in mind two essential principles: first, a teacher's obligation is always to act in the student's best interests; and, second, the closer the student-teacher relationship, the greater the potential for harm when a teacher's sexual intentions enter it.

Spiritual Non-Teachers

It's also important to distinguish spiritual teachers from two other categories of folks who publicly offer spiritual insight.

The first such group is spiritual writers and speakers who neither teach in any formal way nor work one-on-one with people—Karen Armstrong and Harold Kushner, for instance. Typically, such people make frequent public appearances, mostly or entirely before large groups. Such speakers or writers show up, make their presentation or lead their workshop, and leave. There is no building of individual relationships and no one-to-one spiritual intimacy (except, perhaps, for a few moments during a question-and-answer session).

Any one of these folks may be celibate, lovingly monogamous, adulterous, or wildly promiscuous. They may also be deeply aware, very deluded, or both. Some of them (through not Armstrong or Kushner) try to use their fame, eloquence, or cleverness to lure others into bed. While I don't condone this, especially when the speaker or writer violates a vow of celibacy or monogamy, we need to acknowledge this as garden-variety seduction. The most essential features of the teacher-student relationship—one person's immense faith and trust in the other, and the great power differential between the two—don't come into play very much. If a lecturer with great spiritual insight comes on to you, you and they are more-or-less equal adults. You might admire them immensely, and you might also find them very, very hot. Still, you have the power to choose how you'll respond, just as you would with any other attractive person who puts the moves on you. After all, no deep trust or great spiritual intimacy has been established between the two of you.

The second group is people who profess no wisdom of their own but claim to channel ethereal spiritual teachers. This channeling purportedly involves two or more beings cohabiting the same body in a sort of corporeal time-share. Whether such experiences are genuine, pathological, imagined, or fraudulent, the principles of doing no harm and acting in a student's best interests remain equally pertinent. No matter who is ostensibly in charge of a body at a given moment, there must be no sexual power plays, no manipulation of the student for anyone else's gain, and no betrayal of the student's trust.

Some Final Preparations

As you read the chapters that follow, please keep two essential points in mind:

First, my intent in this book is not to prove that I'm right or to make the best arguments. My goals are to advance the larger discussion* on the topic, to inspire students and spiritual teachers to act more mindfully, and to create greater safety and spiritual intimacy between teachers and their students, and within spiritual communities.

Second, I am not against sex, not against seduction, and not against the expression of sexual vitality. I heartily approve of sex, delight in it, and think the world would be better off if there were

---

*This larger discussion continues in the section of this book called "Some Further Questions," as well as on my websites, thespiritualteachersite.com and sexandthespiritualteacher .com.

more of it (within certain moral limitations that I won't spell out here). I don't wish to emasculate or defeminize anyone. Nor do I wish to tame or sanitize sexuality's awesome power.

Indeed, my hope is that, as one result of this book, spiritual teachers and their authentic, loving partners—as well as their students and *their* loving partners—will experience fuller, happier, juicier sex lives filled with immense intimacy and intense joy.

As for those who choose celibacy, my wish is that they will become more settled, serene, and happy in their celibacy.

Chapter 2

Exploiters, Errants, and Exceptionalists

BECAUSE SO MANY spiritual teachers lose their way, at times we may want to abandon the whole bunch. We shouldn't, though. The world's major spiritual traditions have produced great numbers of spiritual teachers who were (and are) mindful, generous, compassionate, and consistently faithful to their vows of fidelity or celibacy—and profoundly helpful to their students.

It's equally tempting to think that all spiritual teachers who have sex with their students share a single essential motive, character trait, or emotional need. They don't. We humans are way too diverse and complex for that.

We can, however, identify and describe three general profiles:

Exploiters scheme, manipulate, or talk their way into students' beds. Their sexual relationships with students are usually planned and deliberate, though sometimes unconsciously so. These relationships are rarely built on a deeply held mutual connection, though the teacher may claim that such a connection exists. Usually, the exploiter simply finds the student sexually appealing, as well as available or vulnerable. Exploiters often try to build harems and/ or spiritual empires; in many cases, their exploitation of students involves not only sex, but money and/or power as well.

When an exploiter vows fidelity or celibacy, it may be only for show. Exploiters' sexual encounters usually involve multiple students (whether simultaneously or in sequence) and a repetitive pattern of behavior.

Errants genuinely value long-term monogamy or celibacy, and they see the wisdom of not becoming sexually involved with their students. Nevertheless, they don't live up to this wisdom, and eventually succumb to temptation. When an errant loses his way, he knows it and, in most cases, promptly admits it.

A sexual relationship between a student and an errant usually involves a unique and mutually felt connection. Often, the relationship arises from a combination of mutual attraction; big stresses in the teacher's life, making him vulnerable; and similar stresses in the student's life. Such a relationship is almost always mutual and consensual. Nevertheless, as we'll see in later chapters, it often creates a great deal of suffering—for the student, the teacher, and their spiritual community.

Exceptionalists are half-brothers (and half-sisters) to errants. They, too, value long-term monogamy or celibacy, and understand deeply why sexual involvement with a student can be so problematic. Also like an errant, an exceptionalist loses his way because of a genuine and mutually felt connection with one of his students. *Unlike* an errant, however, the exceptionalist mentally carves out an exception for his sexual relationship with his student. He believes (or tells himself) that this relationship is in some way unique—and, thus, that it is honorable, wholesome, and not subject to the usual rules.*

One variant of exceptionalism is what we might call double exceptionalism. In such cases, spiritual teachers deeply understand the delusive nature of the exceptionalist mindset, yet get taken in by it anyway, and declare themselves to be exceptions twice over.

---

* Some exploiters have been known to masquerade as exceptionalists—i.e., they talk (and pretend to believe in) an exceptionalist line, but in fact don't believe it at all, and are simply using it to lure students into bed.

For example: "Justine and I are exceptions because we grew up together and were close friends for years before she became my student nine months ago. We're building our romance on the foundation of those earlier relationships, just like when one spouse becomes the other's student. We both know how easy it is to fall into exceptionalist thinking—but we've both looked at this very carefully, and we both agree that our situation really is a legitimate exception. It may look like we're exceptionalists, but we're not. We're exceptions in that way."

Some Common Exceptionalist Excuses

▶ Our motives are pure.

▶ I love the student and the student loves me.

▶ Our relationship goes much, much deeper than any typical romantic partnership.

▶ We both have our eyes wide open. We're being as present and mindful as we can.

▶ We're both in our sixties; we're not star-struck kids.

▶ We've known each other since before I became a spiritual teacher.

▶ We've both been through sexual boundary training and understand the potential dangers and dynamics of our relationship.

▶ I'm not the student's only teacher.

▶ It feels so totally right to both of us. Nothing has ever felt this right to us before.

▶ We're not going to ignore what we both feel is right just because someone disapproves of our relationship.

Zooming in Closer

Within these general categories, we can identify eleven common subtypes of spiritual teachers who lose their way sexually. I'll briefly describe each of these below. The first five subtypes are all exploiters.

- ▶ *Charlatans* claim to be spiritual teachers, but in fact have no spiritual motives or aspirations. They're out to acquire sex, money, and/or power by offering bogus (and, in some cases, even some genuine) spiritual guidance.
- ▶ *Predators* may have genuine spiritual inclinations or aspirations. Nevertheless, they actively and repeatedly—and, in some cases, compulsively—seek sexual gratification from their students. Usually this involves multiple students and brief, casual sexual relationships. In rare cases, instead of actual sexual contact, a predatory teacher will encourage two students to have sex while the teacher watches.
- ▶ *Narcissists* simply follow their own wants and agendas, sexual and otherwise. They pay little or no regard to the needs of their students, the health of their spiritual communities, or the rules, precepts, and tenets of their spiritual traditions.
- ▶ *False Brahmins* believe themselves to enjoy a special status that exempts them from the codes of behavior that other, ordinary folk must follow. False Brahmins feel they are permitted—and, indeed, entitled—to do whatever they please. False Brahmins differ from exceptionalists in that they believe *themselves*, rather than a particular relationship or situation, to be special. Thus they have no qualms about using other folks—including their students—to gratify their own desires.*
- ▶ *Libertines* publicly preach and promote promiscuity among their students—and, usually, between themselves and their

---

* For the record, I don't approve of *actual* members of the Brahmin caste ignoring commonly accepted codes of behavior and doing whatever they please, either.

students. Unlike the previous types of teachers, libertines are not hypocritical, since they follow the same clear (if questionable) codes of behavior they espouse to their students; they're generally not secretive, either. Libertines often use the terms *open marriage* or *polyamory* (sometimes spelled *polymory*), which mean "having multiple sex partners." Libertines tend to do much less harm than other exploiters; in fact, some students who have sex with their libertine teachers don't feel harmed at all, and may enjoy their liaisons quite a bit. However, other students ultimately feel exploited and violated by libertines' casual breach of the teacher-student sexual boundary.

▶ *Serial errants* believe in staying celibate or faithful to their partners, and to honoring the sexual boundary between teacher and student. They also publicly espouse the wisdom of such faithfulness. Despite their declared intentions, however, a serial errant crosses the sexual boundary—and may break a fidelity or celibacy vow—more than once, with more than one student.

▶ *Serial exceptionalists* mirror serial errants, but believe that, in becoming sexual with their students, they have maintained their way rather than lost it because of their unique circumstances.

▶ *One-time, long-term errants* sincerely vow to remain faithful or celibate, or to keep the teacher-student sexual boundary intact. Despite their declared intentions, however, a long-term errant breaks that vow or disrupts that boundary through an ongoing relationship with a student.

▶ *One-time, long-term exceptionalists* similarly break their vow of fidelity or celibacy, or cross the sexual boundary with a student, but feel that their unique situation justifies their actions.

▶ *One-time, short-term errants* sincerely vow to remain celibate or faithful, or to keep the sexual boundary with their students in place. However, they break that vow or boundary once, for a brief period, typically during a time of great stress or personal vulnerability.

▸ **One-time, short-term exceptionalists** also break a vow or boundary once, for a short time, but at the time feel that their unique circumstances make this disruption okay. Later, however, they come to regret their actions.

All eleven subtypes of teachers may (or may not) offer their students a great deal of genuine wisdom and useful guidance. This is true even of some of the most predatory exploiters. This fact is counterintuitive, illogical, bewildering, and even tragic—yet spiritual teachers have proven it true for many centuries. We students ask ourselves, over and over: *How can a spiritual teacher be so wise and yet so foolish, so generous and yet so acquisitive, and so loving and yet so self-centered?*

If we are serious about making our spiritual relationships and communities safer, we need to stop looking for satisfying explanations to this question. We would be wiser to instead accept and deal with the reality behind it. Whether we like it or not, many spiritual teachers *are* both wise and foolish; many *are* both generous and acquisitive; many *are* both loving and self-centered. In fact, a small number of exceptionally insightful and inspiring spiritual teachers have also been serial exploiters; a few have been sociopaths and/or sex addicts.* Our failure to see and accept this is *our* limitation, our delusion—and the more we continue to live by it, the more we enable exploitation and abuse.

One way to look at—and accept—this contradiction is to under-

---

* Philip Roth describes this paradox, which he calls Portnoy's Complaint, in the satirical novel of the same title. The novel's opening page provides this (fictional, yet quite accurate) clinical definition of the condition, as if Roth were quoting a psychology text: "Portnoy's Complaint: A disorder in which strongly-felt ethical and altruistic impulses are perpetually warring with extreme sexual longings, often of a perverse nature . . ." Peter Rutter notes this same paradox in *Sex in the Forbidden Zone*: "[M]ost men who sexually exploit women are in pivotal conflict between the life-giving and destructive sides of their own personalities."

stand that it simply reflects the nature of the human heart, which often operates in utterly contradictory ways. Think of the tough-as-nails corporate raider who melts in the presence of a friendly animal, or the social worker who selflessly supports and fights for their clients, but neglects their own family. Spiritual teachers are no different, for they are human beings with human hearts. We are no different, either, and need to accept these same contradictions in ourselves. Indeed, often our inability to accept fundamental contradictions in others stems from our unwillingness to accept those same kinds of contradictions in our own hearts, minds, and guts.

It's also true that each of us develops along multiple lines—and this development is never equal along all lines. Some of us develop great intellectual powers but little intuition. Some become geniuses in music or art or math or basketball, but can't write a cogent paragraph. Some can give rousing and mesmerizing speeches but are inept at small talk. Some have huge, open hearts, but no clue as to how to run a PowerPoint slide show—or, for that matter, a spiritual institution. And some can have great insight into the nature of existence, yet may be short on empathy, common sense, basic social skills, or the ability to clearly envision the potential consequences of their actions.

Nevertheless, some of us students imagine that our spiritual teachers are less complex or more consistent than other folks. Some of us even imagine that our teachers are more (or better) than human.

We need to stop imagining all of this, because these delusions get us into big trouble. They also harm our spiritual teachers, by encouraging them to join us in those delusions.

Although each spiritual teacher (and every adult human being) is responsible for their own actions, it's also true that the healthier a spiritual community is, the fewer opportunities it will offer its teacher for sexual misconduct, and the more it will sanely support each teacher's monogamy or celibacy. This suggests that, with the right support systems in place, most good spiritual teachers will never become exploiters, errants, or exceptionalists.

In later chapters, I'll discuss what these support systems might look like, and how to build and maintain them.

Beyond Ethical Judgments

In many spiritual communities there has been much hand-wringing about whether teachers who lose their way should be permitted to continue teaching, when their status as clergy and/or spiritual leaders should be revoked, and if and when they should be booted out of their communities. Most of this discussion typically focuses on what is fair *to the teacher*—while the question of what most supports the safety and spiritual intimacy of the community may get overlooked.

Indeed, when a community first learns that its spiritual teacher has had sex with one or more of his students, almost everyone—students, teachers, onlookers, psychologists, writers—typically leaps to moral judgments, and then uses those judgments as the basis for decision-making.

It seems to me that this is a large and fundamental error. Such an approach often leads to endless debates of right and wrong, the teacher's merits and demerits, issues of loyalty, and more hand-wringing. Often the result of all this is a schism in the community. (We'll look at this in more detail in Chapter 23.)

We can argue endlessly about what constitutes ethical or unethical behavior for a spiritual teacher, and what constitutes a fair or unfair response to that behavior. We can also, like Talmudic scholars, split hairs, imagine exceptions, and ask all kinds of "what ifs": *What if the teacher's former partner asks to become his student, and he says yes, but after two weeks they realize they're still deeply attracted to each other, yet during those two weeks he's helped her see what's been blocking her from living wholeheartedly, although she probably would have had the same realization on her own fairly soon, plus she has authority issues with her father...* We can spend years circling in such eddies, trying to come up with a perfect ethical framework, the most effective moral fitness test, or the right place to draw a hard-and-fast line. Yet none of this is going to work very well. The world is simply too alive and varied and uncertain to be nailed down in such a way.

I suggest this alternative approach: we can deal with spiritual teachers' misconduct through two simple and pragmatic concerns—safety and job fit.

Safety is essential to any healthy spiritual community. Indeed, a spiritual community in which some members do not feel safe is arguably neither very spiritual nor terribly healthy.

Spiritual teachers, like physicians, are charged first and foremost with doing no harm. Thus, when a spiritual teacher transgresses (or is accused of transgressing), the primary consideration should always be the safety of the community and its members. Anyone who threatens the safety of one or more community members should be asked to stop—and, if they continue, ordered to leave. It makes no difference whether this person is a drunk ex-boyfriend, a longtime community member who develops borderline personality disorder, or the community's head spiritual teacher. Even a nonhuman threat to people's safety—a rabid dog, or last month's egg salad—may need to be removed for everyone's well-being.

Indeed, in deciding the immediate fate of a teacher who has transgressed, it is often sufficient to ask a single question: "If this person continues as a teacher in our community, is he likely to harm anyone?" If the answer is yes, then the teacher should be required to step down permanently; if it is no, he should either be removed temporarily or permitted to continue on a probationary basis.

This is not Ph.D.-level philosophy. The same question can (and should) be asked about almost anyone in a service role, including bus drivers, teachers, pilots, photographers, and so on.

This approach enables spiritual groups to avoid a common but tragic scenario: while meetings and discussions and deliberations go on for months, the spiritual teacher continues sexually exploiting his student(s).

The issue of job fit is equally relevant. A talented doctor whose right hand becomes paralyzed needs to stop doing eye surgery. I can't—and shouldn't—be a commercial pilot: my vision is simply too poor. My wife, who is five feet tall, is too small to be a firefighter: she can't lug around a fire hose or carry an unconscious person up a flight of steps. In a similar way, some people with immense insight, great compassion, and first-rate presentation skills may nevertheless lack an important quality or skill that a spiritual teacher needs. Amrit connects deeply with her students but has trouble setting boundaries and saying no. Barney is extremely warm and generous, but he's in denial about people's dark and manipulative sides. Corinne often works too hard and pushes herself too far, occasionally leaving herself vulnerable to her own and others' neuroses. None of these limitations is shameful or unusual, even for folks with deep insight. But each can cause (or encourage) a teacher to lose their way. And if the teacher has *already* lost their way, they will be tempted to stay lost, or to lose it again, unless they do the tough work of addressing their own limitations.

One essential quality of any good spiritual teacher is the ability to act consistently in their students' best interests, without regard for their own gain or pleasure or ease. Thus, someone without this ability is simply unsuited for the role of spiritual teacher, and should not be permitted to assume or maintain it.

Who Goes and Who Stays

We thus come to a somewhat startling conclusion: of the eleven profiles described earlier, only the one-time, short-term errant and the one-time, short-term exceptionalist pass the "do no harm" and "best interests" tests. Based on their past actions, teachers fitting *all* the other profiles are likely, sooner or later, to return to having sex with their students. (I'm not suggesting that this is inevitable, only that it is likely.) Thus, spiritual teachers who fit any of the other nine profiles should be removed from their teaching roles.

This is neither the tragedy nor the ignominy many of us imagine it to be. People get fired all the time for not having the appropriate skill set or emotional makeup. These folks don't shrivel up and die;

they find different jobs for which they are better suited. Spiritual teachers who have transgressed can do the same. They can sell cars or shoes or insurance. They can design websites or offices or product packaging. They can answer phones in call centers or questions at airport information counters.

Or, people who cannot be trusted to work one-to-one with students can offer excellent guidance and wisdom as public speakers or writers (but not, of course, as clergy or counselors). In these more public roles, which preclude spiritually intimate one-to-one contact with students, ex-teachers can offer the best of themselves to the world while staying out of situations in which they may harm others.

Nor do spiritual teachers have to wait until such a career change is forced upon them; they can always make such changes themselves. Imagine this scenario: a teacher and his student find themselves deeply attracted to one another, and confess their feelings to each other. The teacher then says to the student, "We can't have it both ways. I can't be both your lover and your teacher. I have to choose, and I choose you. If we're going to be together, you need to find a different teacher, and I need to step down from my teaching role in this community, at least for a short time. I'm willing; are you?" This offers caring and protection for the student, the teacher, *and* the spiritual community.

In discussions about spiritual teachers and sex, we usually assume that sex is a choice, but that a spiritual teacher's role is a given. It's not; it's a choice, too. Indeed, in each moment, all of us—whether we're nurses, webmasters, janitors, homemakers, farmers, writers, or spiritual teachers—make the same fundamental choice: to continue in our current role, and to accept the requirements and limitations of that role, or to give up that role and be free of those requirements and limitations.

Chapter 3

Tangled Webs

THE PATHS involving sex between a spiritual teacher and a student can lead through many different terrains. These paths are sometimes conscious, sometimes unconscious, and, often, partly both.

We can identify and describe eleven such paths. Let's look briefly at each one, from the most to least harmful:

- ▶ *Sexual assault.* Forced or violent sex between spiritual teachers and students is of course quite rare. More commonly, the teacher will begin with some consensual contact—say, a hug—and turn it into something sexual. Out of shock, surprise, or confusion, the student may then become unresistant. Later, if the teacher is accused of sexual exploitation, he may describe this lack of resistance as consent.
- ▶ *Role bait-and-switch.* A one-to-one meeting begins with the teacher in his usual teaching role. As the encounter proceeds, however, the teacher changes its dynamics via sexual energy, talk, and/or touch. Here, too, students' shock or bewilderment may keep them from resisting or leaving.
- ▶ *Sex as a spiritual teaching or tool.* Some teachers present sex with them as an aid to enlightenment or growth—e.g., "This exercise will heal your wounded heart" or "You're so close to seeing your true nature—all you need is one profound experience of nonduality." Others turn *not* having sex

with them into a threat of spiritual failure: "I'm offering you an opportunity to finally let go of your egoistic attachments. If you're too scared to complete the process you began fifteen years ago, that's your business. But I'm deeply disappointed. I expected so much more of you. I thought you were serious about this journey."

▶ *Power plays.* The teacher uses his status, his experience, his awareness of human vulnerability, his knowledge of the student, and/or his spiritual insight to manipulate the student into sexual compliance. Although some power plays can be complex and can involve weeks or months of manipulation, others can be quite simple—e.g., looking a student in the eye and saying firmly, "Take off your clothes and come here," or having an assistant tap a student on the shoulder and announce, "You'll be spending the night with Baba."

▶ *Sex as a prize or honor.* In one variation, the teacher uses sex to confer status on the student. ("I'd like you to be my personal assistant. That means you'll handle my correspondence, keep my office tidy, and be my Beloved One.") In another, the sex is framed as a reward or recognition of status already attained. ("I use this technique only with my most evolved students.") In a third, the teacher presents the sex itself as a gift. ("I want to give you this special blessing.") In a fourth, sex with the teacher is presented as a spiritual initiation or sacred ritual.

▶ *Verbal manipulation.* This is ordinary b.s. tarted up with spirituality. Common variations include *grand destiny* ("This was meant to happen from the day the universe began"; "God promised me He would bring us together some day"), *less-than-grand destiny* ("You know what's going to happen next. Don't fight it; just let go and be one with the experience"), and *what a mess you are* ("I can see that most of your chakras are closed down. That's why your whole life is so out of balance. Do you want me to open them for you—or do you want to stay stuck?"). Some teachers, of course, may employ ordinary b.s. without any spiritual veneer ("You have gorgeous energy").

▶ *Professions of love and/or proposals of marriage.*[*] These can of course be entirely authentic and wholesome. But they are also some of the oldest and most effective tactics that exploiters use to lure people into bed. (Later on, they may rescind their love, or break or deny the engagement.) In other, rare cases, spiritual teachers fool themselves, confusing their desires or neuroses with love.

▶ *Sexual dealmaking.* This is a more-or-less straightforward transaction: the teacher offers time, attention, status, or approval in exchange for sex. ("Yes, you can come to India with me—if you'll share my bed.")

▶ *Ordinary seduction (or ordinary attempted seduction)*, i.e., chatting people up, inviting them in for coffee or wine, leading them to the balcony to look at the stars, offering them a shoulder massage, etc.

▶ *Simple, straightforward offers of sex.* This is libertines' specialty. It can be private (e.g., asking a student, "Would you sleep with me tonight?") or very public (e.g., ending an evening talk by saying, "I'm going to bed. Would someone like to join me?").

▶ *Giving in to mutual attraction.* In one common variation, both people fall willingly into each other's arms; in another, the student successfully seduces the teacher.

It's not hard to see that the first nine of these scenarios are inherently exploitive or manipulative. The tenth—a simple, straightforward offer of sex—is at least honest and no-nonsense. However, as we have seen, even the offer of sex can erode the teacher-student

---

[*] As one spiritual teacher I interviewed noted, "Marriage is not a free pass." Offering to marry someone—or, for that matter, actually marrying them—doesn't magically resolve (or even provide cover for) power inequalities, role confusion, or exploitive inclinations. Indeed, it typically highlights and accentuates them.

sexual boundary, and, thus, reduce the trust and intimacy that are the bedrock of any teacher-student relationship.

Only the last scenario, giving in to mutual attraction, qualifies as errant or exceptionalist behavior.

Excuses and Justifications

Now let's examine—and critique—some of the bogus things spiritual teachers tell their students to encourage or compel their sexual compliance. The list below is representative rather than exhaustive.

- ▶ "It will loosen you up, help you become more open."
- ▶ "I'm filling you with deep spiritual energy" or "I'm opening you to Divine love."
- ▶ "I'm helping you break some of your deepest attachments."
- ▶ "I'm completing (or blasting away) a big piece of your karma."
- ▶ "It's a spiritual initiation."
- ▶ "It's what God wants."
- ▶ "I'm enlightened. I'm not subject to the laws of karma like most people."
- ▶ "I'm acting from a higher plane."
- ▶ "I'm testing your faith. Do you trust me or not?"
- ▶ "I need to find out if *I* can trust *you*."
- ▶ "If you ever expect to learn from me, you must never question me or my actions."
- ▶ "This is how it's been done in my country/sect/culture/tradition for many generations."
- ▶ "To you it looks like abuse or exploitation, but it's not. You don't see what's really happening here, but I do."
- ▶ "I'm acting out of nonduality."
- ▶ "I'm worshipping the One in you."
- ▶ "I'm beyond lust" *or* "I have no desires."

▶ "It's just energy going from one part of the universe to another."
▶ "There's no doer; there's just doing. There is no 'you' or 'I,' so how can there be abuse or exploitation?"
▶ "It's a spiritual teaching."
▶ "It's crazy wisdom (or left-handed tantra or skillful means)."

All this exploiter talk has two things in common: first, a disregard for the needs and concerns of the student, and, second, a failure to openly acknowledge the teacher's own desires, and his attempts to fulfill them. These add layers of narcissism and dishonesty atop the exploitation and manipulation.

On the following pages I look briefly at each of these excuses; explain how and why it is bogus (or outright cheesy); and, in some cases, suggest an appropriate reply. Despite the occasionally snarky tone, I'm deeply serious about everything I say and suggest.

A Student's Reality Check

SPIRITUAL TEACHERS' BOGUS REASONS WHY YOU SHOULD HAVE SEX WITH THEM

▶ *"It will loosen you up, help you become more open."* So will twenty minutes of hatha yoga or ninety minutes of massage. So will a self-induced orgasm. If all the teacher can offer is loosening and opening, he's not much of a spiritual teacher—and a lousy lover.
▶ *"I'm filling you with deep spiritual energy"* or *"I'm opening you to Divine love."* You're *already* filled with deep spiritual energy and Divine love; they're why you got interested in spirituality in the first place. And—as spiritual teachers from all major traditions

have pointed out for many centuries—you already have full access to these; you don't need to get them from someone else. Either the teacher knows this and is exploiting your innocence, or he doesn't and he's a fraud.

▶ *"I'm helping you break some of your deepest attachments."* True. Attachments are typically broken by painful, disillusioning experiences, and the teacher is about to provide some. This teacher could also help you loosen your attachment to money by swiping your wallet, or to your health and appearance by pushing you in front of a moving car.

▶ *"I'm completing (or blasting away) a big piece of your karma."* Perhaps. And adding a big new piece to the karma pile.

▶ *"It's a spiritual initiation."* Spiritual initiations are fine, but they don't need to involve sex with the teacher. Ask for the initiation without the sex; if the teacher insists that the two are inseparable, turn down both.

▶ *"It's what God wants."* The teacher assures the student that sex with him has been approved by the Absolute. This takes two common variations: (1) "It's okay for us to have sex—we were husband and wife in a previous life." (Does this mean that if you were my servant in a previous life, I can order you around? Or, if I was your guard dog in a former life, I can come to your home and bite strangers?); (2) "I've prayed to God long and hard about this, and He's given us His blessing to sleep together." (What if the teacher prays even longer and harder, and God gives him His blessing to have sex with your kids, too?)

- *"I'm enlightened. I'm not subject to the laws of karma like most people."* Ask the teacher to demonstrate this by running naked across six lanes of heavy traffic. Or, if you're in a more gracious mood, remind him that *you* are fully subject to the laws of karma—and, for the sake of your own karma, you need him to back off. (In any case, how does a teacher's enlightenment—whether real or imagined—enable you to avoid cause and effect? It's like saying, "I'm a brilliant mathematician, so you're not subject to the laws of physics.")

- *"I'm acting from a higher plane."* Maybe, but you're getting exploited and manipulated on *this* plane. Encourage the teacher to have sex with someone on that other plane instead.

- *"I'm testing your faith. Do you trust me or not?"* Correct answer: "Not anymore."

- *"I need to find out if I can trust you."* Implication 1: the best (or only) way to find out if someone is trustworthy is to ask them to have sex with you. Implication 2: if the person does have sex with you, they're trustworthy; if they don't, they aren't. This would make prostitutes and their customers the most trustworthy people on the planet—and celibates and whistle-blowers the least. In saying this, the teacher has actually proven that *he* is not trustworthy.

- *"If you ever expect to learn from me, you must never question me or my actions."* Don't be like Moses, Buddha, Jesus, Muhammad, Lady Julian of Norwich, Martin Luther, Martin Luther King, Jr., Mother Teresa, or the Dalai Lama—all of whom questioned spiritual authority. Be more like Eva Braun, who never questioned the actions of the man she so deeply admired.

▸ *"This is how it's been done in my country/sect/culture/tradition for many generations."* Possibly true. But this justification has been used for centuries to support clitorectomies, widow burning, racism, anti-Semitism, the binding and crippling of young girls' feet, the murder of newborn girls, and mass murder.

▸ *"To you it looks like abuse or exploitation, but it's not. You don't see what's really happening here, but I do."* Translation: "Don't trust your own heart, mind, or gut. Instead, trust me. Now take off your clothes and fuck me."

▸ *"I'm acting out of nonduality."* How does acting from nonduality justify exploitation or manipulation? Would it be okay if the teacher broke into your home, trashed it, and punched out your kids, so long as he did it out of nonduality?

▸ *"I'm worshipping the One in you."* Worshipping the One in you (or anyone) is great, but it certainly doesn't require sex. Say yes to the worship and no to the sex.

▸ *"I'm beyond lust"* or *"I have no desires."* (1) This is probably a lie. (2) How does being "beyond lust" or "having no desires" justify sexual exploitation? Would it be okay for your teacher to spit on you if he assured you he was beyond salivation? (3) What does being "beyond lust" even mean? (4) Especially when the speaker has an erection.

▸ *"It's just energy going from one part of the universe to another."* By this definition, so are pushing a pie into the teacher's face, spraying him with seltzer, or putting a poisonous spider down his shirt. Ask him if he's okay with your doing these things.

▶ *"There's no doer; there's just doing. There is no 'you' or 'I,' so how can there be abuse or exploitation?"* This is the cheesiest dodge of all. True, in Absolute terms, there's no doer or doing, no good or bad, no right or wrong, no life or death, no pain or pleasure, no consent or exploitation—in fact, no specifics of any kind; everything is One. At the same time, though, we also live in the relative realm, where we need to pay our taxes and lock our doors; where people sometimes try to manipulate us; and where we need to protect and defend ourselves from such folks.* This excuse is particularly foul—and particularly transparent—because it can be used to justify anything at all: rape, torture, genocide, even the destruction of all life on Earth. Indeed, centuries ago it was used to train samurai to become ruthless, guiltless killers.

▶ *"It's a spiritual teaching."* This excuse has so many ramifications that I've devoted an entire chapter (Chapter 18) to it.

▶ *"It's crazy wisdom (or left-handed tantra or skillful means)."* This boils down to "it may look selfish and manipulative, but it's for your own good." This, too, merits a full chapter of discussion (Chapter 20).

---

*The Absolute and relative realms are in fact identical—but that's not a discussion to have here.

There's a second set of justifications that we would also be wise to examine: other people's. Typically, once a scandal breaks and a spiritual teacher's integrity is cast into doubt, a variety of folks will rush to support and defend him. These typically include some of the teacher's students, colleagues, and family members, as well as some members of his inner circle (if he has one). Here are some of their common excuses and justifications:

▶ *"You have no right to judge him. Stop judging people. Judging isn't spiritual. Look at yourself instead."* In fact, we all have a right—and an obligation—to judge people's motives and actions, and to decide how to respond to them. That's why we give money to certain charities (and certain panhandlers) but not others; why we smile at some strangers but not at others; and why we choose our sexual partners instead of having sex with everyone who asks us to. Judging—i.e., being discerning—is not only spiritual, but necessary. As for looking at your own actions and decisions and habits of mind, that's always a good practice for all of us.

▶ *"He's a powerful and charismatic man. Sex is an expression of his spiritual power. You can't have one without the other."* The issue isn't the teacher's expression of his sexuality, but sexual involvement with his own students. Unless he's vowed celibacy, he is free—and, indeed, encouraged—to be a stallion with a partner who is not his student. In any case, it's nonsense to say that if you have power and charisma, you also have to have sex. Think of the great contemporary Christian figures who have remained celibate—e.g., David Stendl-Rast, Thomas Keating, and Mother Teresa. Or consider the great contemporary Buddhist figures who also have stayed celibate—the Dalai Lama and Thich Nhat Hanh, for instance.

▶ *"He's human like the rest of us. We all make mistakes."* True. If we're wise, though, we publicly acknowledge them, apologize for them, learn from them, accept their consequences, and don't repeat them.

▶ *"So he made some mistakes. You have to balance the damage he did against all the good he did."* This is a legitimate way to review the life of someone who has died. But someone who is still alive has the potential to do further good—and further damage. We need to continue to hold ourselves, and each other, accountable for our present and future actions. No matter how much good someone has done, that doesn't entitle them to exploit others, now or in the future.

▶ *"What's the problem? It's a fair trade. He gets sex; I get to be around him all the time. I love basking in his aura. And now most of his other students treat me like royalty."* This may indeed be a fair trade. But the teacher, the student, and their spiritual community should honestly recognize the nature of this relationship: that of an alpha figure and his concubine. (I'll say much more about alpha figures in Chapter 11.)

Spiritual Culture Clashes

In some cases, sexual relationships between spiritual teachers and their students are framed as cross-cultural misunderstandings. Such misunderstandings, we are told, commonly occur when a spiritual teacher from one country or culture teaches students from another.

It's not hard to see how, years ago, non-Western spiritual teachers with little knowledge of Western cultures sometimes misinterpreted their students' friendliness, directness, and revealing outfits. Some teachers were shocked; some didn't know how or where to set their personal boundaries. Others thought they were being offered casual sex—and perhaps sometimes they were.

In another common example, the exact opposite occurred: a teacher freely dispensed hugs or other forms of friendly, nonsexual touch—and this shocked, offended, or shook up folks.*

---

* Differing expectations, mores, and personal boundaries don't just create friction across

Now, however, because of increased mobility and the ubiquity of the Internet, television, and cell phones, many of us know a good deal about cultures and traditions other than our own. Thus, spiritual teachers who travel to foreign cultures and countries can and should be far more savvy than they used to be about what they are likely to encounter, and how to act in response. We can also reasonably expect the folks who arrange and sponsor teachers' trips to be knowledgeable about cultural differences, and to make sure that visiting teachers are culturally well prepared.

So, these days, when a spiritual teacher has (or attempts to have) sex with one of his students, and then tries to chalk it up to a "cultural misunderstanding," the excuse is entirely unconvincing.

Sexual Addiction

Sexual addiction (sometimes called sexual dependency or sexual compulsivity) is an inability to manage one's sexual behavior. Sex addicts typically feel compelled to engage in promiscuous sexual encounters, often with strangers or prostitutes. Other forms of sexual addiction include compulsive masturbation and the compulsive viewing of pornography. Debate rages among psychologists, physicians, and other professionals as to whether compulsive sexual behavior is a genuine addiction, like alcoholism or narcotics addiction; whether it is a variant of obsessive-compulsive disorder; or whether it is a disorder at all. Some clinicians, such as Aviel Goodman, suggest that certain people may be neurologically predisposed to sexual addiction. Whatever its causes and provenance, however, sexual addiction is real and thrives among us.

We students often believe that great spiritual insight and sexual addiction (or, indeed, any addiction) are mutually incompatible. We think, *Surely anyone with such wisdom would recognize the*

---

cultures and religious traditions; they can also cause problems *within* a single culture or tradition. In some Muslim and Jewish sects, for example, *any* bodily contact between a man and a woman is prohibited unless they are spouses or blood relatives.

painful consequences of addictive behavior and be able to hold themselves in check.* Once again we are ignoring reality and clinging to a cherished ideal. Not only do some spiritual teachers suffer from sexual addiction, but a few have become notorious for their compulsive sexual encounters, which typically involve their students.

Many of us take this delusion further. We think that spiritual insight can somehow prevent or cure all psychological (and even physical) ills, including those that have neurological or biological roots. In real life, though, spiritual teachers can and do experience mental illnesses, personality disorders, Alzheimer's, dementia, ulcers, cancer, and pretty much everything else. (Some students and teachers carry this delusion further still, into the realm of physical injury. When one spiritual teacher was injured by a New York City cab that strayed onto the sidewalk, he was surprised that such a thing could happen to him.)

But spiritual insight does not somehow destroy all of a teacher's neuroses, moral blind spots, goofy ideas, and difficult temptations. (However, the wisest teachers have relatively few of these, are aware of most of the ones they do have, freely admit to them, and take care to adjust for them as necessary.)

One common feature of addiction, including sexual addiction, is denial. Certainly most of the justifications and excuses presented earlier in this chapter can be used in service of this denial. So can excuses without any spiritual claims, such as "I live a Bohemian lifestyle" or "I refuse to be bound by the Victorian morals of this sick, bourgeois society."

Hard as it is for some of us to admit that our teachers have normal human limitations, it's harder still to accept that they may have addictions, compulsions, depression, or stress-related illnesses. Yet it's essential that we (and our teachers) do admit it. Otherwise, *we* are in denial, and we become enablers, part of sick teachers' addictive systems.

---

* It's worth noting that "willpower trumps addiction" is itself a dangerous fantasy.

Chapter 4

Creating Healthy Teacher-Student Relationships

AT THE CENTER of every healthy teacher-student relationship are several implicit agreements:

- ▶ The student hopes to become wiser, more aware, more loving, and/or more fully human.
- ▶ The teacher commits to helping the student in this endeavor, and to acting in the student's best interests at all times. This includes not harming or exploiting the student in any way. (It may, however, sometimes involve telling the student some difficult or painful truths—or, in service of something greater, sometimes doing the opposite of what the student hopes for or expects.)
- ▶ The student trusts that the teacher will honor these commitments.
- ▶ The *student* also agrees not to exploit the *teacher* for their own emotional, sexual, or financial gain.

When honored, these agreements create a rich soil in which trust and wisdom can grow. When these agreements are not fully honored by both sides, however, trouble can easily arise.

In any healthy teacher-student relationship, both people are adults who are fully responsible for their own actions and decisions. Spiritual teachers can guide us, encourage us, and tell us when we are full of crap. But they are not—and should not be—our surrogate parents. In fact, some of the most troublesome issues between spiritual teachers and their students typically arise when we try to make them into our surrogate parents, or project our own parental or authority issues onto them.

The Dance of Power

Any teacher-student relationship is based on a mutual awareness that the teacher knows more about certain aspects of human life, and the human heart, than the student. In some ways, this naturally creates a power differential between any spiritual teacher and their students.

At the same time, however, spiritual teachers have only as much power as we students give them. We always have the option of ignoring them, disputing them, or walking away. By trusting and paying attention to spiritual teachers, we make their teaching possible. Without us, they'd have no one to teach.

Part of our job as students, then, is to give our teachers the right amount of power. This means allowing them to influence us, perhaps quite deeply—but not allowing them to brainwash us, control us, or make us smaller or less human.

In practice, this means subjecting everything a teacher says to our own careful scrutiny. As you attend to a teacher's words and actions, do they seem right to your heart, your gut, and your head—or do they feel off the mark? Do they seem accurate and wise, or confusing or senseless? Do they emphasize that the teacher is every bit as human as you, or do they imply that the teacher is more or better than human? Does the teacher consistently serve your (and other students') best interests, or do they appear to serve or gratify themselves? It's essential to wrestle with what any spiritual teacher says, writes, and does, and to hold all of it up against the light of your own best judgment.

Scrutiny isn't an insult to any teacher. On the contrary, it's a way to take them—and yourself—seriously. The more insightful a teacher is, the more your scrutiny will validate what they say, and the deeper their teaching will sink in.

Questioning or challenging a teacher is a vital part of any healthy student-teacher relationship. When something a teacher says doesn't hold up to your careful observation, it's important to question them, challenge them, or ask them to help you refine your understanding. This enables you to go deeper and get clarification—and, when a teacher's response falls short, it gives you a better feel for their weaknesses and limitations. It also gives the *teacher* a better sense of how *you* think and feel.

We of course need to scrutinize our teachers' actions as well as their words. We can learn a great deal from insightful and compassionate teachers simply by observing what they do. We can also spot our teachers' weaknesses, and notice if and when they don't live by any principle they preach.

As we observe what a teacher says and does, we would be wise to ask ourselves this essential question: *Does their behavior follow and uphold the essential principles of human connection, compassion, and service?* And if anything the teacher does seems amiss, we can also ask: *Would I accept these actions from my doctor or dry cleaner? Would the police and courts accept them from my doctor or dry cleaner?*

Another excellent way to observe and evaluate a spiritual teacher is to get to know their students over a period of weeks or months. A sane, loving, and wise teacher will mostly have sane and loving (though not necessarily wise) students; a teacher with limited insight or personality problems will tend to attract like-minded students.

If we don't scrutinize what a teacher says and does, or if we fail to exercise our own good judgment, we don't just harm ourselves; we also harm the teacher, by encouraging their arrogance, narcissism, or delusion. As John Kain writes in *A Rare and Precious Thing: The Possibilities and Pitfalls of Working with a Spiritual Teacher*, "Being in the teacher role is a powerful position, and, like heroin, such power can be addictive. As students, we often fuel this addiction by giving over our power to the teacher; we become enablers, co-conspirators."

The Boundary Paradox

Spiritual teachers often help their students break down, see through, or transcend boundaries—between opposing parts of themselves, between themselves and others, between themselves and the Absolute, and so on. Furthermore, as our teachers work with us, we let them deeply affect our hearts, guts, and heads—even our dreams. Yet in our relationships with these teachers, we're told and expected to "maintain healthy boundaries."

This paradox pervades our lives and lodges deep in our bellies. We need to be vulnerable if we are to open our hearts, yet we need to protect ourselves in order to stay sane, healthy, and safe. We need to take the risk of being hurt—yet we need to also block out people and forces that would harm us. This is precisely why spiritual teachers' sexual transgressions sometimes hurt us so deeply.

This paradox is another potent manifestation of the Absolute/relative paradox I discussed earlier: we live in a universe that is both unitary and seemingly made up of innumerable separate entities. In fact, the word "universe" derives from the Latin *universum*, meaning "all things combined into one."

Like most spiritual paradoxes, no words or concept will explain this away or remove its sting. We must each resolve it for ourselves through living our lives, making and learning from our mistakes, and growing in wisdom day by day and breath by breath. Yet it helps to acknowledge that it *is* a paradox—and a part of living a spiritual life.

Still, some useful general things can be said about personal boundaries between spiritual teachers and their students.

As we have seen, student-teacher relationships often closely resemble those of therapist and client, and are usually much more intimate than those of clergy and congregants. It's not unusual for a spiritual teacher to probe, challenge, or ask questions that might sound rude or invasive coming from an ordinary spiritual leader. Furthermore, in discussions, spiritual teachers and their students can get into some intensely intimate stuff—about trust, love, sex, family, money, hopes, fears, regrets, yearnings, beliefs, assumptions, ontology, epistemology, soteriology, and how to live a decent or meaningful life.

But within each teacher-student relationship, the teacher must always put aside their own desires and agendas, and do whatever is in the student's best interests. This inspires trust, which doesn't—and shouldn't—grow overnight. Usually it is a slow and protracted process. A wise teacher does not hurry things, but lets this trust grow naturally, and rewards it at each step with insight, compassion, and service.

As students, when we sense that our teachers are focused on our best interests, we can allow our trust in them grow. But if we sense that a teacher is not supporting our spiritual well-being, we can and should create some emotional distance. This may mean asking questions:

- ▶ "What are you thinking right now?"
- ▶ "Why did you ask me that?"
- ▶ "What are you doing?"
- ▶ "Why are you moving our discussion to that topic?"
- ▶ "Is there something you want or expect from me?"
- ▶ "Why are you touching me?"

It may also mean saying no:

- ▶ "I'm not okay with talking about that."
- ▶ "I'll think about this topic some more, but let's not go any further down that road right now."
- ▶ "That's too painful for me to look at right now; maybe later."
- ▶ "Please don't touch me."

▶ "If you do that again, I'm leaving."
▶ "I don't care how ancient a tradition this is; I need you to stop right now."

It may even mean physically leaving the situation, asking the teacher to leave, or pushing him away.

This is a matter of discernment, of trusting and following your gut. Ultimately there is no script to follow, no printed chart to consult—and you are (and must be) your own final authority.

Chapter 5

The Spiritual Teacher
as Role Model

"SPIRITUAL TEACHER" is not just a role or job title or career path; at its best, it is an active, living expression of mindfulness, service, and love. When spiritual teachers live an awake and loving life, they encourage us, inspire us, and help us to do and be our best. They also remind us what we are capable of.

Since spiritual teachers help us become more fully human,* there's never a time when they're "off duty" as role models. If a spiritual teacher regularly expounds on serenity and compassion but sometimes beats his dog, we (correctly) consider him a hypocrite. Ditto for the teacher who holds his students to a higher standard than he holds himself. We can and should expect that our spiritual teachers live admirable and ethically consistent lives—just as we would with judges, police chiefs, and ordinary clergy.

In practice, of course, no spiritual teacher is perfect;† like all human beings, teachers will make occasional mistakes and have some limitations and failings. At times we'll see them lose their

---

* Any teacher who offers to help you become more than human is deeply deluded, fraudulent, or both.

† If a teacher claims that they're perfect or infallible, run like hell in the other direction. But if a teacher says *everything* is perfect (or whole, or complete, or just the way it has to be), they may be pointing to the Absolute rather than acting out of egotism or delusion.

tempers, argue with their partners, wear mismatched socks, or eat three Snickers bars before dinner. If they're decent and authentic teachers, though, they'll readily and publicly admit their mistakes and limitations, and, when appropriate, apologize and make amends. They'll also say "I don't know" when they don't know.*

Spiritual teachers should thus neither hide their flaws nor indulge in them to the point where they harm their students. We students, in turn, should neither expect our teachers to be perfect nor cut them so much slack that we encourage them to lose their way.

Although spiritual teachers can teach us a great deal about living wise and compassionate lives, this doesn't mean we should become exactly like them, especially in matters of culture or taste. Acting, talking, or dressing like your teacher doesn't imbue you with their wisdom, any more than imitating Denzel Washington's personal habits turns you into a great actor. Indeed, we shrink rather than open our hearts when we become our teachers' clones, puppets, or wannabees. We don't do our teachers any favors, either. We each need to be authentically ourselves—just as we need to let our teachers be authentically themselves.

Spiritual Teachers as Sexual Role Models

We students need to insist that our teachers express their sexuality wisely and lovingly—just as we expect them to be generally wise and loving in all other aspects of their life. (In the case of celibate teachers, we need to insist that they *contain* their sexuality wisely and lovingly.)

But we should not be prudes or prigs. We need to let our teachers have their sexuality, in all its glory and variety. A monogamous teacher and their loving, monogamous partner are entitled to

* Some contemporary spiritual teachers, such as Adyashanti and the late Seung Sahn, have insisted that not-knowing *is* our essential dynamic with the world. Similarly, the fourteenth-century Christian text *The Cloud of Unknowing* describes "a cloud of unknowing that is betwixt thee and thy God." Eight centuries before that, when the Chinese emperor asked the Buddhist sage Bodhidharma, "Who are you?" Bodhidharma replied, "Not knowing."

explore the vastness of the sexual landscape, so long as no harm or exploitation is involved.

If and when an unpartnered spiritual teacher begins a sexual relationship with someone (i.e., someone from outside their spiritual community), they would be wise to quickly introduce their new partner to the community. "This is my new partner Lin, whom I'm wild about. I hope you'll treat Lin warmly, the way you already treat me." Such prompt disclosure discourages rumors and gossip; it also begins to open a place for the teacher's new partner in the community.

We students, in turn, would be wise to promptly acknowledge and get past our quasi-parental feelings ("He can do *so* much better than her"), and to accept our teacher's partner for who they are, rather than who we hoped or expected them to be.

We also need to accept that spiritual teachers will have a wide range of views and teachings about sexuality. Some teachers deliberately emphasize the strength and sacredness of sex; others treat it as nothing more than a normal part of life, like loving our children. Some teachers practice—and teach couples—meditative, spiritual, and ecstatic approaches to sex. Others practice, emphasize, and/or encourage celibacy. Still others don't say much about sex at all.

Because spiritual teachers are our role models—including, in part, our sexual role models—their sexual misconduct doesn't just undermine our trust in them; it also corrodes our trust in *ourselves*. A voice in our heads says, "If even my teacher can't stay monogamous (or celibate), then how can I?" Monogamy or celibacy may suddenly seem unsustainable, and our teachers' actions encourage us to follow in their footsteps.

Chapter 6

Why Spiritual Teachers Are Sexy

MOST DISCUSSIONS OF SEX between spiritual teachers and their students focus on power, projection, boundaries, coercion, accountability, etc.—the stuff psychologists talk about at conferences. They're all legitimate, important topics, but they can seem weak and tepid compared to the hot power and pressure of sexual desire.

It's true that spiritual teachers and their students do get sexually involved because of projections and transference and illusions and fantasies and old emotional tapes. But let's not ignore or deny the obvious: they also do it because they turn each other on.

So let's declare, loudly and clearly: *Spiritual teachers are often very sexy, usually in multiple ways.* Here are some of those ways:

Spiritual teachers are often wise. Wisdom is sexy.

Many spiritual teachers are eloquent speakers and/or brilliant thinkers. Eloquence, intelligence, great thoughts, and deep insight are all sexy.

Spiritual teachers often wear cool, sexy clothes such as robes or prayer shawls. Often these are black (the coolest, sexiest color) or white (arguably the second sexiest). Some teachers who wear ordinary suits often wear expensive, beautifully tailored ones. Spiritual teachers from other cultures may dress exotically (to our eyes), and exotic clothing is usually sexy.

Many spiritual teachers are well known or outright famous. Fame is deeply sexy.

Spiritual teachers are powerful—certainly within their communities, and sometimes in the world at large. Power is extremely sexy. High status, a corollary of power, is sexy, too—and spiritual teachers typically have high or very high status in their spiritual communities. Alpha status, which I'll discuss in detail in Chapter 11, is sexier still.

Many spiritual teachers have charisma. Charisma is fabulously sexy.

Spiritual teachers make many people—especially their students— feel deeply known and understood. This is extremely sexy.

Some spiritual teachers are sexy simply because they're handsome or beautiful. They'd be sexy even if they had little spiritual insight, and were piano tuners, pipefitters, or librarians.

When the people around us consider someone sexy, we're more likely to find that person sexy, too. In spiritual communities, this feedback loop can make some spiritual teachers extremely desirable.

And spirituality itself can be sexy. Indeed, sexual and spiritual ecstasy share many common traits.* Both are experienced deep in the body, in rushes of energy, pleasure, or joy.

Let's also loudly and clearly declare that it's normal for spiritual teachers and their students to feel *spiritually* attracted to each other—and, indeed, to genuinely love each other, though in a nonsexual way. Over time, however, as trust and intimacy grow between the two people, this spiritual attraction occasionally grows into sexual attraction as well.

We may also become sexually attracted to our spiritual teachers in less conscious or overt ways. For example, to our unconscious

---

* There is, of course, far more to spirituality than ecstasy. In fact, some spiritual traditions and teachers consider spiritual ecstasy to be a beginner's experience with little meaning or import. Other teachers and traditions see spiritual ecstasy as a potential distraction or trap.

mind, our spiritual teacher represents wisdom, compassion, truth, enlightenment, the Absolute, love, our own deepest spiritual impulses, and/or our own best selves. We admire what our teacher represents and we deeply desire it for ourselves. Sometimes we come to physically desire the teacher as well. We may even imagine that physically (i.e., sexually) possessing the teacher will enable us to acquire or experience that same wisdom, compassion, etc. We may also assume that someone who is in touch with the Absolute—someone who is able to touch our deepest spiritual places—must surely know the right way to touch us physically.

Sexual attraction to a spiritual teacher is, like so many other aspects of genuine spirituality, deeply paradoxical. A relationship with a spiritual teacher often feels both deeply intimate and deeply safe. This safety and intimacy are themselves extremely sexy and alluring. They can make us want to give ourselves—spiritually, sexually, or both—to our teachers, so that we can be surrounded (or penetrated) by this great intimacy and safety. Yet were we to actually give ourselves away sexually—and were the teacher to take us—that very safety and intimacy would be largely destroyed.

Let's also remind ourselves that, in general, we human beings are a horny bunch. Indeed, as Christopher Ryan and Cacilda Jethá note in their book *Sex at Dawn*, humans are the horniest complex creatures on the planet. In any twenty-four-hour period, most adults, including many who have taken vows of celibacy, find themselves sexually attracted to dozens of people. At times, most of us are briefly sexually attracted to people other than our spouses or partners; to our bosses and co-workers; to some of our close relatives; and to our spiritual teachers.

We needn't deny any of this attraction, or tell ourselves that it's wrong or bad. Nor should we demand that our spiritual teachers frump themselves down, or act cold or distant, to protect us from our own feelings of attraction. Instead, we would be wise to let ourselves feel this attraction fully—and then to let it go without acting on it.

In short, we students need to let our spiritual attraction to our teachers bloom, while keeping the *expression* of our sexual attraction to them in check. This is neither as difficult nor as unusual as it sounds. We hold ourselves similarly in check all the time with friends, close relatives, co-workers, and acquaintances.

Lastly, just because spiritual teachers have the lion's share of power in their relationships with students, this doesn't mean *we* are free to act out, sexually or otherwise—and of course it doesn't mean they are, either. A student who flirts with their teacher or tries to seduce them only weakens the teacher-student relationship—and if the seduction is successful, it can blow that relationship to pieces.

Chapter 7

Sex and Spiritual Experience

THE WORLD'S spiritual traditions are hugely divergent, and deeply conflicted, on the subject of sex. Depending on which tradition, sect, or spiritual teacher you consult, you'll learn that sex is a wondrous, holy, and life-affirming force—or an enervating distraction that dissipates our energy and destroys our spiritual focus. You'll discover that sex can be sacred, demeaning, profane, transcendental, or ordinary—and that it should be forbidden, suppressed, enjoyed, indulged, transmuted, or transcended. (This divergence isn't unique to sex, of course. Our various traditions and teachers provide an equally divergent range of responses to most important aspects of human life.)

Our many traditions, sects, and spiritual teachers are equally conflicted about what constitutes spirituality. Is it loving our neighbors? Shooting energy up our spines? Feeding the poor? Meditating alone for a month? Praying for peace? Speaking in tongues? Honoring our parents? Doing yoga (and, if so, what kind)? Making a pilgrimage to Mecca, the Ganges, or Jerusalem? Volunteering at the local nursing home? Not eating animal products? I know two spiritual teachers who refuse to use the words "spiritual" or "spirituality" at all, and insist that all meaning has leached out of both words.

The phrase "spiritual experience" is equally problematic. What makes an experience spiritual? The way it feels? The insight it provides? The degree to which it transforms us—and if so, transforms us into what? Is a powerful, soul-shattering vision a spiritual experience? What about the slow, subtle realization over the next several months that this vision was high in energy but low in insight? What about the realization that you've spent your life habitually chasing after spiritual realization?

Some spiritual teachers, especially those in the yogic traditions, teach a variety of "spiritual" exercises that create states of bliss, typically by redirecting energy flows in the body. These states are quite real, and quite delightful. But are they spiritual? If so, are they more spiritual than a good workout at the gym, or an hour spent on the beach, gazing at waves?

Can sex with your lifelong partner be a spiritual experience? How about casual sex with an attractive stranger, if it's approached mindfully and with a generous spirit? If your whole body buzzes for ten minutes, and you have a huge, screaming orgasm, but nothing much happens for your partner, did you have a spiritual experience, while your partner did not? What if the sex fizzles out, but the two of you feel tremendously close and content? What if your whole body buzzes for ten minutes, and you have a huge, screaming orgasm—all while masturbating?

For that matter, what constitutes a *non*spiritual experience? Eating lunch? What if you eat it mindfully? What if it's with a group of homeless people whom you help feed at a soup kitchen? What if you're one of the homeless people? What if you're one of the homeless people, but you eat mindfully?

Because such questions create an endless loop of confusion, we might do better to ask ourselves some different ones. I suggest these: *Does the proposed action or choice create more understanding or empathy? More generosity? More openness? Does it reveal or deepen connections with people? With the world? With the Absolute?*

Meanwhile, no matter what questions we ask ourselves, real life presents us with difficult, ever-changing, moment-by-moment choices. Some of these are choices about sex and spirituality that will have consequences for real human hearts, minds, and bodies.

The Big Spiritual O

Many of us come to spiritual teachers feeling like virgins who long to lose our spiritual virginity. Often we believe that the right spiritual teacher can give us, or lead us to, a powerful "spiritual" experience. In essence, we look for a teacher who will bring us to spiritual climax.

Some of us also come to spiritual teachers in the expectation, hope, or belief that they will make us complete—or teach us how to complete ourselves. We admire in our teachers those personal qualities we want to develop ourselves, and may feel that we currently lack. We may also project onto our teachers the ability to fulfill us—as if they will somehow do our internal work for us.

This may have a familiar ring because it's how we often approach new and potential romantic partners. Yet, just as in romance, these attitudes set us up for disillusionment and disappointment.*

Many of us who place ourselves in spiritual teachers' hands are primarily looking for "powerful" or "profound" or "peak" experiences—i.e., the spiritual equivalent of orgasm. We imagine that experiencing truth or the Absolute must involve a physical or emotional jolt, like a wave of energy washing through us, or a blast of energy up the spine, or a feeling that our third eye or crown chakra is opening. The bigger the effect something has on

---

* I should add, though, that many spiritual teachers assign great value to disillusionment and disappointment. Georg Feuerstein goes a step further: he suggests that people on authentic spiritual paths are the ones *most* likely to experience disappointment, disillusion, shock, and despair. Mariana Caplan goes further still: "The path of disillusionment is one of the most potent and instructive roads we can follow. It is the path of compassion through humility." And Jack Kornfield agrees: "Disillusionment is an important part of the spiritual path. It is a powerful and fiery gate, one of the purest teachers of awakening, independence, and letting go that we will ever encounter."

our body, the more profound we think it must be. And if an experience doesn't have a physical or emotional kick to it, it must not be truth—or, at least, not a truth worth experiencing. In short, we expect our truth to be hot and juicy.

Some spiritual teachers offer their students these kinds of experiences. Other teachers, however, dismiss them as unimportant—the stuff of spiritual beginners.* Some even view such experiences as distractions, dangers, or potential addictions. What is the fundamental difference, these teachers ask, between getting a buzz from a joint, or a double espresso, or a set of "spiritual" exercises? They warn students that they can easily get stuck in blissful or "powerful" experiences, yearning to repeat them again and again, like a cocaine addict who needs to keep doing lines.

Truth vs. Thrills

People on spiritual paths tend to fall into three general groups: truth seekers, thrill seekers, and comfort seekers. To some degree, all of us have all three orientations—but in most of us, one of the three clearly predominates. Our focus may, of course, change over time; many folks who start out looking for thrills or comfort eventually turn to seeking truth.†

In the pages that follow, I'll discuss the first two of these groups: truth seekers and thrill seekers.

Truth seekers want to get to the bottom of things. They are willing to experience difficulty, pain, despair, disappointment, exhaustion, and boredom, if that's where the scent of truth leads them.

---

* Zen and insight meditation teachings, in particular, are full of stories of excited students reporting their insights and blissful states to their teachers, only to be told, "Oh, yes, that's a common side effect. It doesn't mean anything. Just ignore it." As Zen teacher Steve Hagen notes, awakening doesn't feel at all profound or powerful, but simple and natural. Instead of a blast of energy, it's more likely to be experienced as profound relief.

† Some spiritual teachers scoff at the very idea of looking for truth: "Why look for it? We already live in it. It's like looking for light on a sunny day."

But they're not masochists, ascetics, or prudes: if the smell of truth wafts through sex or gourmet cooking or running a business, they'll follow it into those realms just as willingly.

In contrast, thrill seekers go after peak experiences. These may be physical, emotional, sexual, or all three. Thrill seekers sign up for workshops on tantric sex, astral travel, power yoga, kundalini awakening, and whole-body orgasm.

Sexually, spiritual thrill-seekers tend to lean toward two extremes:

1. those who consider sex a path to the Absolute
2. those who consider celibacy, and the *supplanting* of sexual energy and bliss with spiritual energy and bliss, to be a path to the Absolute

Both of these paths have long and venerable histories in multiple spiritual traditions. Both, however, are quests for ecstatic experience—and both mirror the quest to find a partner who can give us a huge, dramatic orgasm.

Ultimately, any quest for spiritual thrills boils down to acquisitiveness and a desire for self-gratification. Some spiritual teachers call these thrills "spiritual toys" or "spiritual candy." Some also call the pursuit of these thrills "spiritual materialism," which is fundamentally not very different from hedonism.

In the twenty-first century, when we can gratify far more of our physical and psychological desires than ever before, the promise of "spiritual fulfillment" (however it might be defined) is deeply alluring.* Having become jaded with all the goods, services, culture, and sex we can acquire, we want still more. "Spirituality" is the perfect upping of this ante—partly because it promises thrills of a higher order, partly because we can claim to be "spiritually advanced" even as we chase after those thrills.

This approach can easily lead to an unhealthy dependence on

---

* Some spiritual teachers insist that "spiritual fulfillment" is a contradiction in terms. The very act of seeking fulfillment, they insist, gets between us and truth.

a spiritual teacher who we believe can give us—or withhold from us—powerful "spiritual" experiences. It can also make us easy marks for teachers with less-than-noble intentions, since they can dangle all kinds of shiny spiritual objects in front of us, and promise them to us as rewards if we do what they say. This approach can also make us feel frustrated and disgruntled—or like spiritual failures—when the spiritual highs stop coming. And we can end up stuck in an endless loop of searching and grasping for the next big spiritual experience.

The biggest drawback to spiritual thrill seeking, though, lies not in its potential frustration, but in its fulfillment—in actually having some high-voltage spiritual experience.

When thrill seekers have such an experience, they are often convinced that they have had a huge spiritual breakthrough: profound enlightenment, a transformative mystical vision, an encounter with God, an experience of nirvana, a visit to the Pure Land, full-blown *kensho*, etc. This is like thinking someone must be your soulmate because they brought you to a huge orgasm. To spiritual thrill seekers, though, the depth, significance, and authenticity of the experience seem self-evident. How can something so "powerful" be anything but a great spiritual opening? They *must* have achieved something incredible, deeply important, and well beyond "ordinary" spiritual experience.

Some thrill seekers who have such an experience imagine themselves to have been singled out by God or to have attained an especially high level of wisdom. Emboldened by this delusion, they declare themselves to be spiritual teachers and begin taking on students of their own.

Such teachers are often charismatic, confident, and very sexy. Yet they are usually profoundly mistaken about their own insight. Because of their confusion of voltage and wisdom, their teachings often emphasize "having your own powerful spiritual experiences" or "breaking open your spirit" or "evolving to ever-higher states of bliss," etc. Often these teachers believe that they can give or induce such experiences in their students. Thus these teachers become both gatekeepers and purveyors of their students' "spiritual development."

All of this tends to be very attractive and exciting for other spiritual thrill seekers. As a result, these teachers can quickly become very popular. Their spiritual communities are often unhealthy, however, and some turn into cults.

Such a teacher is especially likely to lose their way sexually, and to become a false Brahmin. Their confidence and charisma make them sexually very desirable. Meanwhile, their arrogance and delusion cause them to think of themselves as special. Over time they may talk themselves into transgressing with arguments like these: "I earned it. Where would this student be without me?" "I deserve it. I'm special." "I've had a unique spiritual experience. The normal rules don't apply to me." "I've sacrificed so much in this role. This is my just reward." Such teachers set themselves up for a big fall—one that may also take down the whole spiritual community.

The history of religion brims with examples of such teachers and spiritual leaders. But we are not doomed to repeat these mistakes endlessly. Mariana Caplan has written a magnificent book on the subject, *Halfway Up the Mountain: The Error of Premature Claims to Enlightenment*, which I strongly recommend to every student and every spiritual teacher. In this book, and in her *Eyes Wide Open: Cultivating Discernment on the Spiritual Path*, Caplan helps readers to build their powers of spiritual discernment, and to learn to separate wisdom from delusion.*

Spiritual thrill seeking has one other notable quality: it tends to burn itself out. Some people who are more interested in thrills than in truth ultimately dump religion altogether and take up hang-gliding, or mountain-biking, or the Landmark Forum. Others wake up to what they've been doing and realize that spirituality has little to do with self-gratification.

---

* Let's not assume that Caplan is the queen of discernment, however. She has had her own failures of discernment, including spiritual and romantic ones, and is quite open about them. She even wrote a one-act musical comedy, *Zen Boyfriends*, based partly on them.

Chapter 8

The Paradox of
Masculine Sexuality

EACH OF US has a sex (the organs between our legs), a gender (the sexual identity between our ears), and a sense of masculinity or femininity (a set of attitudes, experiences, and behaviors).* Our sexuality is a combination of all three—part nature, part nurture.

How much is nature and how much nurture? Which elements of our sexuality are socially constructed, and which ones are in our genes? There are more positions on these questions than there are legs on a caterpillar, and the arguments for and against each one fly thick and fast.

Most of this chapter sidesteps these arguments—and for the discussion that follows, we don't need to sort through and evaluate them. We simply need to focus on the ways in which many men (and some women and transgender folks) actually think and feel—and the ways in which their thoughts and emotions can encourage them to transgress.

---

* As Leslie Fiedler, Anne Fausto-Sterling, and others have pointed out, human beings have more than two sexes. Fielder, the author of *Freaks* and many other books, identifies seven; Fausto-Sterling, the author of *Sexing the Body* and *Myths of Gender*, suggests that there are five. The sexes we call male and female, however, are far more common than other physical configurations, such as a vagina plus a scrotal sac but no ovaries, or a vagina and ovaries plus a penis. Psychologist John Money, a specialist in the study of congenital sexual-organ defects, suggests that up to 4% of all people are born intersexual.

I call this welter of forces *the masculine psyche*, but that's nothing more than a handy term. If you feel it's more accurate to say *how men are wired* or *what makes men tick* or *the heteronormed expression of male dominance as played out through unconscious drives, learned behavior, and the promulgation of cultural stereotypes*, by all means substitute your term for mine as you read.

Masculinity is not a one-size-fits-all proposition—and neither is sexuality. The terms *masculine sexuality* and *the masculine psyche*, as I use them here, don't fit all men. They do fit many men quite well, other men less well, and some not at all. They will also, in part, fit some women and some transgender people. In cases where this particular shoe doesn't fit, don't try to jam it on. Don't think I'm trying to jam it on, either. The discussions that follow are intended solely as tools for understanding—not as constricting boxes in which all men are forever stuck. (For readers who are interested in learning more about masculine sexuality and energy, I strongly recommend David Deida's insightful book *The Way of the Superior Man*.)

Why spend an entire chapter examining the masculine psyche, while largely skipping over the feminine? Simply because sexual transgression is *far* more common among male teachers than among female ones—as we saw in Chapter 1, by a ratio of twenty-four to one. We can't entirely chalk this up to male privilege and hegemony. Something else is going on. I propose that, in large part, it goes on in masculine hearts, minds, guts, and genitals.

The more clearly we see the masculine psyche, the more skilled we can become at working with (or, if necessary, around) it—no matter what sex or gender we are.

Let's zoom in for a close look.

Checking Out the Masculine Psyche

These useful general observations can be made about the masculine psyche:

The masculine psyche wants to have sex with multiple partners. In a 1992 study of "private wishes"—i.e., things people secretly wish for—men and women wished for very similar things, with one notable exception: men consistently wished "to have sex with anyone I choose." This preference cut across all samples and age groups, including happily partnered men.

The masculine psyche treats sex as a commodity—something to be consumed, like a meal or a movie or a game of golf. Men often view attractive people as potential sex delivery systems, and sex as an activity other people can provide to us, in the same way that a pizza delivery person can provide us with dinner. Thus heterosexual and bi men often objectify women, and gay and bi men often objectify other men.

Masculine sexuality yearns to conquer and acquire. The masculine psyche gets a big thrill from using its power (e.g., its skills, wit, status, intelligence, physical force, etc.) to sexually conquer others. Some men express this by sexually conquering as many people as possible; others, who are happily monogamous, enjoy conquering their partner over and over. In many men, the desire for sexual conquest and acquisition is mirrored—or, sometimes, supplanted—by urges to acquire as much fame, status, money, respect, adulation, and/or "spiritual advancement" as they can.

The masculine psyche compartmentalizes sexual feelings. Many of us men can actively dislike someone, yet simultaneously be very turned on by them. In the masculine psyche, sexual arousal can occur side-by-side with almost every other emotion, including anger, grief, despair, fear, and boredom.

As part of this compartmentalization, many men live by a sexual morality that is at odds with their other moral standards. History is replete with men of otherwise high moral character who slept around, or kept mistresses or concubines, or attended orgies, and so on.* Exhibit A is Martin Luther King, Jr.—but spend a little time on Google and you can readily dig up Exhibits B through Z.

---

* I refer here to men who, so far as we know, lived otherwise wholesome lives. History is,

To the masculine psyche, sex is a strong and reliable palliative. If we're feeling bad for any reason, many of us will reach out for sex in order to feel better.

Although sex can be an expression of intimacy for anyone, *to the masculine psyche, sex can* create *intimacy where there hasn't been any.*

To the masculine psyche, the right visual stimulation can be very sexually arousing. A glimpse of flesh, a photograph, or even a drawing can be sufficient. (To many of us, including me, Jessica Rabbit is hot—and she's a cartoon character.)

Many men spend a good deal of time providing their own visuals—i.e., fantasizing about sex. Even when men are deeply committed to their partners, these fantasies often feature attractive strangers, acquaintances, and/or imaginary people who have been sexually objectified.

In an initial encounter with another person, the masculine psyche typically does an immediate, split-second evaluation of that person's sexual attractiveness. This often determines how the evaluator will treat that person. If the person clears the attractiveness bar, the evaluator may then make an equally quick judgment of that person's potential availability as a sexual partner *(Are they in or out of my league? How are they responding to me? Are they wearing a ring?).* Even men who are happily partnered habitually follow this script. Family therapist Thomas Wright puts it this way: "In judging someone's suitability as a partner, for men physical attractiveness is the first cut."

To the masculine psyche, sex is a great ego boost. Sex can make men feel powerful, confident, virile, and, afterward, fulfilled and at peace. Sex with a new partner adds an additional ego boost: the thrill of conquest and acquisition.

The masculine psyche often perceives sexual desire as an almost-separate entity: an impersonal, amoral craving, like a strong wind or wave, that clamors for equally impersonal satiation.

---

of course, even more replete with men of ostensibly high moral character who, when not in the public eye, transgressed in a wide variety of ways.

To the masculine psyche, sex is one of the most important elements of life—perhaps the *most important element.* Many men cannot imagine living without sex. Some men, faced in midlife or late life with loving partners who no longer sexually desire them (or whom they no longer sexually desire), abandon their partners for new ones who are more attractive or sexually available—often creating great suffering in the process.

Masculine sexuality often feels called to follow a familiar script: find an attractive person; seduce them (or otherwise sexually acquire them); have sex with them (and, perhaps, impregnate them); abandon them; repeat the process ad infinitum.

Many men are particularly aroused by the crossing of a sexual boundary. Peter Rutter suggests that "for men sexuality is often most intense when it is most forbidden." Paradoxically, the more respect some men have for others' personal boundaries, the more they may also yearn to violate them. Rev. Grant Bennett, who became sexually involved with a member of his congregation, puts it this way: "I understand the need for a boundary, but there is an incomparable excitement in the possibility of going across it. I don't know why it's so important, but it is."*

If crossing one sexual boundary is incomparably exciting for some men, it may be more exciting still for a partnered or celibate spiritual teacher to have sex with his partnered or celibate student, thus violating three sexual boundaries at once. There's a painful irony here: men with little respect for others' personal boundaries

---

* In *The Betrayal Bond*, Patrick J. Carnes offers this explanation for why Rev. Bennett and some other helping professionals feel such incomparable excitement: "Some professionals (clergy, physicians, attorneys) will have sex with those entrusted to their care (parishioners, patients, clients). Some in these professions develop a pattern of high-risk sex that is clearly addictive. Most were sexually abused as children and learned to connect their sexuality with fear. So as adults, they feel most sexual when it is dangerous or risky. One of the characteristics is that with each episode they take greater risk—until they are inevitably caught." I would add two caveats to Carnes' observation: First, he is describing only one subclass of exploiters; most exploiters, and nearly all errants and exceptionalists, don't fit this profile. Second, Carnes writes only of actions—the actual crossing of sexual boundaries—not of the *desire* to do so. The desire itself, when not acted upon, is not inherently problematic.

will often readily cross them—while some men with great respect for those boundaries will also feel a strong urge to cross them.

On a subconscious, symbolic level, the masculine psyche wants to impregnate everyone and everything—women, men, animals, the ground, the ocean, the whole planet. It yearns to fill the universe with its masculine essence and bring forth new life, just as trees scatter their seeds.

Masculine sexuality tends to operate in these ways regardless of people's spiritual training, cultural conditioning, or beliefs about sex. Some of the impulses we've looked at are heavily reinforced—and, in certain cases, partly created—by relentless cultural messages. But other impulses retain their power *in spite of* strong cultural, religious, and personal messages to the contrary.

Given all of this, *the masculine psyche is, to a large degree, haunted by its own sexuality.* For many of us, our sexuality is a source of many ongoing conflicts. The most common and enduring of these conflicts involves fidelity: many of us go through life firmly committed to a partner (or to celibacy), yet regularly feel tempted to stray.

The impulses described above make up only a part of the masculine psyche. It routinely experiences a great many other drives and impulses, some of which directly contradict each other. For instance, many men want to have sex with multiple partners; many others, however, want to do precisely the opposite: bond with a single partner and love, sustain, and protect them. Many of us simultaneously want to do both.

Indeed, paradox and contradiction rest at the very center of the masculine psyche. Many of us want to conquer our partners, yet we also want to protect them from being conquered or harmed by others. We want to win their affection through our virtue and wisdom, and we want to take them by storm (or seduce them through our power and charm). We want to care for them, and we want to overpower them. We want them to blossom like a flower, and we want to break them open like a shell. We want to give to them and serve them, and we want to control and use them. We want to stay and sustain them, and we want to mate and run. We want to uphold sexual boundaries and we yearn to cross them.

The Role of Testosterone

Although there are many different explanations for how the masculine psyche develops, everyone agrees that one of its major elements is biochemical: the hormone testosterone.

Some folks think that testosterone explains everything about why spiritual teachers lose their way sexually. "Well, of course they lose their way," these people say. "They're almost all men, right? They can't help themselves. It's the testosterone." The assumption here is that when testosterone speaks, men's only option is to hear and mindlessly obey.

Other people say something that sounds similar, but means precisely the opposite. "They're almost all men, right? They have no self-control. When testosterone speaks, instead of covering their ears, they turn up the volume and pull down their zippers." The assumption here is that we can easily ignore testosterone's call, but that we routinely choose not to.

What, then, is the authentic relationship between the masculine psyche and testosterone? Let's take a look at some details.

Healthy men and women both produce testosterone—but, from adolescence on, males produce ten to twenty times as much as females. Andrew Sullivan, author of *Love Undetectable* and several other books, observes that testosterone "profoundly affects physique, behavior, mood, and self-understanding.... It affects every aspect of our society, from high divorce rates and adolescent male violence to the exploding cults of bodybuilding and professional wrestling." A 1993 study showed that men with high testosterone levels were more likely to have failed marriages than those with low or normal levels.

High testosterone levels correlate very closely with masculine thinking and behavior, regardless of people's genital configurations at birth. When Stanford researchers injected newborn female rats with testosterone, their clitorises grew into penises, and they tried to have sex with other females; when male rats had their testosterone chemically blocked, they offered themselves to females in receptive, passive ways.

Since we can't—and clearly shouldn't—perform similar experiments on our fellow humans, we don't have a study demonstrating that human testosterone has similar effects. But we do have good anecdotal evidence that this is so.

In 1999, for example, Drew (formerly Susan) Seidman underwent the lengthy process of changing biologically from a woman to a man. This included testosterone injections every other week. Within two months, Seidman stopped menstruating and began to develop a variety of male physical characteristics. More notably, however, Seidman's thoughts, emotions, and impulses changed. "My sex drive went through the roof. I felt like I had to have sex once a day or I would die." He also became very aroused by visual stimuli, such as the sight of an attractive woman. As a result, he became "*really* into porn."

Andrew Sullivan is himself a fascinating case. When Sullivan was in his mid-thirties, his testosterone levels shrunk dramatically as a result of a long-term HIV infection. To address the problem, he injected himself with testosterone every other week, as Seidman did. Sullivan describes its effects this way:

> I can actually feel its power on an almost daily basis. Within hours, and at most a day, I feel a deep surge of energy. It is less edgy than a double espresso, but just as powerful. My attention span shortens.... My wit is quicker, my mind faster, but my judgment is more impulsive.... And then after a few days, as the testosterone peaks and starts to decline, the feeling alters a little. I find myself less reserved than usual, and more garrulous. The same energy is there, but it seems less directed toward action than toward interaction, less toward pride than toward lust. The odd thing is that, however much experi-

ence I have with it, this lust peak still takes me unawares. It is not like feeling hungry, a feeling that you recognize and satiate. It creeps up on you.... You realize more acutely than before that lust is a chemical. It comes; it goes. It waxes; it wanes. You are not helpless in front of it, but you are certainly not fully in control.

In his essay "The He Hormone," Sullivan writes eloquently on his experiences with injected testosterone, as well as on some of the most intriguing and eye-opening research on the subject. Here are his most trenchant—and slightly chilling—observations:

This, then, is what it comes down to: testosterone is a facilitator of risk—physical, criminal, personal. Without the benefits of testosterone, the cost of these risks might seem to far outweigh the benefits. But with testosterone charging through the brain, caution is thrown to the wind.... It is about the ability to risk for good and bad; to act, to strut, to dare, to seize. It is about a kind of energy we often rue but would surely miss. It is about the foolishness that can lead to courage or destruction, the beauty that can be strength or vanity.

Many observers who examine testosterone and the masculine psyche thus come to the conclusion that men—and, arguably, women and transgender people with high testosterone levels— are inherently incapable of fidelity. "It's not in men's nature to be monogamous." "Men are wired to have sex with lots of different partners." "The masculine essence needs to spread itself in multiple directions, planting its seed in as many places as it can." Sometimes these phrases are intended as accusations, sometimes as apologias, and sometimes as excuses.

Certain folks, male and otherwise, surely *are* incapable of fidelity—either to a partner or to a vow of celibacy—just as some of us are sterile and some of us can't carry a tune. But to argue that *all* men—or all people with high testosterone levels—can't hold steady to a vow, or to a monogamous relationship, is absurd and corrosive. The hundreds of millions of men who stay faithful to their partners demonstrate otherwise. Indeed, history is replete with men who stayed consistently faithful to their partners, or to their vows of celibacy.

The masculine psyche often does yearn to sexually transgress. But there's nothing about masculinity, or testosterone, that *requires* us to lose our way sexually. As Sullivan wisely observed, we are not helpless. The excuse "the testosterone made me do it" simply isn't accurate, though "the testosterone made me really, really *want* to do it" may sometimes be.

For all their intensity and apparent urgency, sexual desires—like all desires—are just passing clouds. They come and go, wax and wane. If we feel them fully and don't grab on to them—and don't try to run from them, deny them, or disown them—they eventually drift away on their own.

The masculine psyche has many voices that call us to sexually transgress. Let them call. We can hear and acknowledge those voices without following them.

Indeed, all of us do this on a regular basis. Our heads echo with all kinds of voices—voices that urge us to steal, to hurt, to fight, to conquer, to destroy, to serve, to protect, to assist, to support, to love, and to do all sorts of other things. We can choose not to follow any particular voice—especially if it urges us to do something harmful, dangerous, or foolish.

I began this chapter by mentioning a study that showed how most men want to have sex with anyone they choose. I admit that I want this, too. Also, I want to go to my favorite restaurant and order everything on the menu. I want to walk into my neighborhood bookstore and say to the manager, "I'll take one of everything." I also want the time to read them all. I want to be a rock star. I want to be five pounds thinner and twenty years younger.

There's a vast gulf between our desires and our actions.

We needn't be slaves to our desires. We don't have to throw ourselves into their arms and whisper, "Take me." We can accept them, hold them lightly, and let them go. We can also place a higher value on wisdom, compassion, commitment, and service.

Our Teachers' Psyches

As we have seen, biologically, mentally, and emotionally, our spiritual teachers are fundamentally the same as the rest of us. Those with masculine psyches also have the same desires and impulses as most men.

Each of these teachers, like each of us, can choose to respond to a desire or impulse in any of several ways:

- ► Follow it. This can create immense suffering.
- ► Argue with it. This only adds to its energy.
- ► Deny, ignore, or shame it—or try to snuff it out or tamp it down. This temporarily weakens the voice, but guarantees its eventual reappearance in much stronger (and sometimes perverse) form, typically during a time of great stress or vulnerability.
- ► Let the voice yammer on; feel its yearnings fully; choose not act on it; and let it go, again and again. This is the one option that actually works—and that can create great sanity for teachers and safety for their students.

Spiritual teachers can't work sexual miracles on themselves. They can't, for example, turn off their sexual desires indefinitely. But wise teachers *can* have a saner relationship with their sexuality than most people. They can be more mindful, less compulsive, less selfish, and less caught up in the cycle of sexual tension and its relief.

Wise teachers can also more clearly see the enormous suffering that sexual misconduct can create. In addition, they can spot, usually well in advance, the actions and decisions that could tempt them to lose their way—and they can choose to act or decide otherwise.

Chapter 9

Common Pressures, Projections, and Temptations

VERY FEW spiritual teachers begin their teaching careers by plotting to have sex with their students.* Most teachers who lose their way fall into their transgressions over time, usually under very difficult or tempting circumstances. Sometimes their own arrogance or delusion plays a big role as well.

However, every spiritual teacher faces a welter of difficulties and temptations that encourage sexual misconduct. The more these are publicly recognized and acknowledged—by both teachers *and* their students—the less likely teachers are to give in to them.

Some of these temptations are quite overt, some more subtle and insidious. Nevertheless, it's teachers' responsibility to stay alert for them; to dodge or deflect (or, if necessary, flee from) them when they appear; and to keep their sexual and other personal boundaries firmly in place.

It's also *students'* responsibility to be as aware as possible of

---

* Though there have been some notable exceptions: In one memorable case, which Alan Lew describes in his book *One God Clapping*, Lew is given this advice by a well-known swami: "...I should drop everything and come study with him, that he would make me rich, and that I would get laid all the time. 'You should have seen the knockers on the woman I was just with in Boston,' he said." Lew chose to not follow the swami's lead.

these temptations and difficulties, and to keep their own boundaries in place as well.

Here are the most common temptations and challenges a spiritual teacher faces:

- ▸ students' immense vulnerability
- ▸ some students' extreme credulity and suggestibility
- ▸ students' misapprehensions about spiritual insight and enlightenment
- ▸ students' idealization of the teacher—in particular, their mistaken belief that the teacher can do no wrong
- ▸ students' transference of their hopes, fears, desires, and expectations onto the teacher*
- ▸ students' tendency to recreate—or act as if they are living through—situations and patterns from their past
- ▸ students' desire to heal old wounds—and/or their compulsion to deepen them
- ▸ students' authority issues—especially their desires to obey, to disobey, to surrender, to defy, or even all four at once
- ▸ students' control issues: their desires to hold on, to let go, and/or to control the teacher
- ▸ students' need to feel special, validated, or deeply understood
- ▸ the teacher's immense power within their spiritual community
- ▸ the teacher's transference of their own hopes, fears, desires, and expectations onto the student
- ▸ the teacher's isolation and loneliness (Paradoxically, the larger a teacher's community is and the more time they spend with its members, the more alone they may feel. This loneliness is not neurotic, but is built into the teacher's role: as someone at

---

* *Transference* is what some forms of psychotherapy call the transferring of our past emotions onto someone in the present. Transference keeps us from seeing the person as they are; instead, we see them through our own past and projections. When a spiritual teacher does any of these things in relation to a student, or a therapist does them with a client, it's called *countertransference*.

the top of the group's spiritual hierarchy, they may have few or no peers or confidants within the group.)

- ▸ the teacher's hormones
- ▸ the teacher's position as a spiritual alpha figure (this is the subject of Chapter 11)
- ▸ students' wielding of their own sexual power (this is the subject of Chapter 12)

Widely known spiritual teachers face additional stresses as well. Typically, they work with many students in multiple locations, and do a great deal of traveling. This can be both wearying and lonely, and it may expose these teachers to an especially large number of opportunities for misconduct.

In addition, each teacher has their own unique vulnerabilities and weaknesses. Although these vary widely from teacher to teacher, the two most common ones are spiritual arrogance (the subject of Chapter 13) and what psychologists John Welwood and Robert Masters call spiritual bypassing: "using spiritual ideas and practices to sidestep personal, emotional 'unfinished business'; to shore up a shaky sense of self; or to belittle basic needs, feelings, and developmental tasks, all in the name of enlightenment."

Most honest and well-intentioned spiritual teachers can skillfully handle many of the above temptations at once. But when most or all of them are piled on together, the weight can feel crushing.

It's a common misunderstanding that spiritual teachers should be able to easily handle almost *anything* that gets thrown at them, no matter how stressful or difficult, under all circumstances. Behind this is the larger and more pernicious delusion that someone who is wise, enlightened, or spiritually advanced is somehow superhuman. They aren't.

Some students use this very delusion to abdicate some of their responsibilities in their relationships with spiritual teachers. They tell themselves that they don't need to set boundaries, be mindful of their teachers' time and energy, or generally act like adults—since, after all, as enlightened beings, their teachers are above such petty concerns.

Yet any healthy relationship between a spiritual teacher and a student is by definition adult/adult, not adult/child. We harm our teachers—and ourselves—when we act like adolescents or children in our dealings with them.

It's certainly true that spiritual teachers will sometimes smile tolerantly at things that would set our own teeth on edge. But that doesn't translate into an invitation for us to act out. Surely our teachers are entitled to the same basic respect and consideration that we would give to receptionists, mechanics, and post office clerks.

In any case, that tolerant smile doesn't mean the teacher isn't bothered—only that they're able to keep their cool in the moment. Later on, in private moments with their partner or trusted friends, they may complain big time. (I can attest to this, having listened to many such complaints from friends who are spiritual teachers.)

Each spiritual teacher must decide how to best handle the myriad pressures and temptations they face. However, they don't have to handle them alone—nor should they.* They can—and ought to—ask for the help of friends, colleagues, professional counselors, and/or their partner. Chapter 29 suggests several ways to make this help more available and accessible.

In short, no teacher needs to feel trapped or overwhelmed by these difficulties and temptations. Teachers can turn to one or more of their support people. They can share how they feel—and openly discuss their limitations and difficulties—with their spirituality community, as I discussed in Chapter 5. And they can fully feel the seemingly overwhelming emotions, then simply watch them without acting on them, until those feelings dissipate like morning mist in the sun.

---

* If a spiritual teacher reaches the narcissistic conclusion that they don't need anyone else's help, this is a harbinger of much misery and havoc to come.

Chapter 10

The Power of No

ONE OF THE MOST important tools a spiritual teacher can wield is the word "no." A teacher who has trouble saying no will soon be eaten alive by the demands of their students and community.

Some spiritual teachers give too much of themselves, say "yes" too often, and balk at saying no. Often this is simply because they are generous folks, and want to be as helpful as they can. Sometimes, though, this generosity can have an element of neurosis: they may feel guilty saying no, or they may be unrealistic about the amount of time and energy they can give.

Some teachers are so generous with their time, energy, and attention that they routinely deplete themselves. Although they may maintain their regular spiritual practices—meditation, prayer, study of texts, etc.—they may not take the time to fill themselves up again through leisure, exercise, solitude, extra sleep, and other forms of self-care. Some may even cut back on their spiritual practices as well.

Ultimately, spiritual teachers—and all people who regularly serve others—need to make a strong, enduring commitment to their own sanity and well-being. Keeping this commitment means being able to say no, sometimes over and over, with compassion and empathy—and without guilt or equivocation. Keeping this commitment ultimately benefits everyone.

The effects of saying "yes" too often and "no" too infrequently can ripple out well beyond spiritual teachers themselves. Teachers who give too much to their students may give too little to their partners or families. Their families, in turn, may feel disappointed, hurt, angry, or resentful.

Part of becoming a functional adult is learning how and when to say no. This ability is triply important for spiritual teachers. Without it, they can easily be blindsided by manipulative students, difficult situations, or even their own emotions. This can be particularly problematic when it comes to sex.

Most spiritual teachers set clear and effective sexual boundaries with their students early in their teaching careers, and these boundaries usually serve them well for the first few years. However, as teachers become better known, several things tend to happen: their community grows, their status as an alpha figure increases, and so does their sexual desirability. More and more students may push against their sexual boundaries—and may push harder, more cleverly, and more insistently. The teacher may also find that the voice of an internal false Brahmin begins speaking to him—perhaps louder and louder. One day the teacher may discover that the boundaries that were adequate for so many years will no longer suffice, and need to be greatly reinforced.

For example, for years a teacher might regularly invite students over for dinner, or go out with them for coffee after talks; as the teacher's reputation grows, however, they may feel the need to draw a clear formal line between friends and students, and will abruptly stop socializing with their students. Another teacher may decide to no longer accept phone calls and visits from students at home. Yet another may stop meeting informally with students, and begin requiring advance appointments.

Yet even this reinforcement of personal boundaries may work only temporarily. As the teacher's star continues to rise—especially if they publish books or speak around the country or world—the pressures and temptations will probably become stronger, more frequent, more profuse, and more insidious. As a result, they may need to regularly set ever-stronger and ever-clearer boundaries,

especially sexual ones. Teachers who don't may one day find themselves in big trouble.

This is not just a problem for spiritual teachers. As Peter Rutter
observes in *Sex in the Forbidden Zone*, "Success itself puts a man
at higher risk for feeling that he can make his own rules and that
his word (or his fabrications) will be believed against the word of
a [victim] who challenges him. In most of the case histories I gath-
ered for this book, the man who had a sexual relationship in the
forbidden zone had been considered an outstanding member of his
profession."

It thus appears that the helping professionals with the *most*
training, education, experience, and renown are, in general, more
likely to have sex with their clients than new and inexperienced
ones. To my knowledge, we don't yet have a study that shows why
this is so. However, it seems clear to me that, as spiritual teachers
grow in status and ability, they attract more students or clients, are
considered more sexually desirable, and are sexually tempted more
and more often. Yet they may fail to steadily strengthen their sexual
boundaries against the ever-rising temptations, both external and
internal. Eventually those inadequate boundaries may break, at
which point the teacher loses his way.

Chapter 11

The Spiritual Teacher as Alpha Figure

AN *ALPHA* (or *alpha figure*) is the top dog of a group, organization, or community. They're the person all its members follow and look to. As John Alexander, author of *How to Become an Alpha Male*,[*] puts it, "Any time people are following you, you've got alpha status." Some groups have a single alpha figure; others have multiple alphas, who form a ruling class.

By definition, spiritual teachers are the alpha figures of their spiritual groups and communities. These groups may also have presidents, executive directors, boards of directors, and so forth, but these folks are usually high-level operational staff. The serious power typically rests in the hands of the top spiritual teachers. (Spiritual teachers who are well known as speakers, writers, workshop leaders, and/or media guests may also have alpha status in their denominations or traditions, in larger religious or spiritual circles, and/or in the world at large.)

There are some notable exceptions, however. Kripalu Center for Yoga and Health and the San Francisco Zen Center, for example,

---

[*] Alexander's book is not a work of psychology, sociology, or anthropology, but a guide for men on how to seduce women. Nonetheless he is as insightful as he is street-smart on the subject of alpha/beta/omega dynamics.

very deliberately do not have one head teacher, in order to avoid the problems associated with having a single alpha figure at the top. Both organizations understand these problems from painful experience: in the past, both were led by very strong alpha figures whose behavior got them and their organizations into very hot water.

For years the term *alpha* was used only in the context of a group. For someone to be an alpha, they needed at least one follower— and usually many. Recently, though, the word *alpha* has been given a second definition, one linked to behavior and personality rather than intragroup dynamics. In their book *Alpha Male Syndrome*,* Kate Ludeman and Eddie Erlandson describe alphas in just such a way:

> Wherever they are and whatever they do, they stand out from the crowd, usually leaving an indelible impression on those whole lives they touch.... Courageous and self-confident, they are turned on by bold, innovative ideas and ambitious goals, and they pursue their objectives with tenacity and an urgent sense of mission.... Often charismatic figures who command attention, they exert influence even when they're low-key and inconspicuous.

As examples, Ludeman and Erlandson offer up (among many others) Michael Dell, Jack Welch, Martin Luther King, Jr., Michelangelo, Josef Stalin, and Saddam Hussein. John Alexander's definition of an alpha is strikingly similar: "confident, social, powerful, outgoing [and] secure in himself."

In animal species, a group's alpha figure is the one most sought after as a potential mate, precisely because the alpha has the most power and status. This is equally true in human groups, but most

---

* Ludeman and Erlandson use the term *alpha male* androgynously, in the same way I use *alpha figure*. Under Ludeman and Erlandson's definition, Angela Merkel and Queen Latifah are both alpha males.

of us would frame the situation differently, by saying that alpha figures are very sexy. They are sexy *because* of their positions at the top of their communities. However, those who also have alpha personalities are doubly sexy. And those who are also physically handsome or beautiful are triply sexy.

How a spiritual teacher manages this sexiness makes a huge difference in what becomes of them, their students, and their spiritual communities. As Ludeman and Erlandson observe, when alpha personalities "are at their worst, they go down in flames and drag their coworkers, their families, and their organizations with them.... We've observed that many leaders who fit the dysfunctional alpha male typology fall prey to sexual predation, becoming womanizers* who use conquest and control to assert their dominance. Their magnetic charisma and take-charge personalities can make them exceptionally attractive, creating temptations that challenge even the most loyal of spouses and—as we've seen repeatedly—cause everyone from religious leaders to heads of state to throw caution to the wind."

Ludeman and Erlandson have thought this through a good deal further. They identify four types of alphas. Three of these—the commanders, strategists, and executors—are naturally drawn to business and politics. A fourth type, visionaries, are often entrepreneurs such as Steve Jobs and Bill Gates; in other cases, however, they become charismatic, and often sexually wayward, spiritual teachers.

For men there is yet another piece to alpha status. Many men report being raised to believe that they were born with special talents, promise, or karma.† Often this includes a sense of destiny and/or entitlement. This encourages males to become alphas; it also encourages narcissism, delusion, and the false Brahmin attitudes described in Chapter 2. Instead of admitting to themselves that

---

* Given the authors' androgynous definition of *alpha male*, we can assume that "womanizers" also refers to men who sexually exploit men, and women and transgender people who sexually exploit folks of any sex.

† This study was conducted in the United States. We don't yet know how widely this sense of male privilege and destiny is shared across cultures and sub-cultures.

they are simply trying to acquire the most power, money, and sex, these men may tell themselves that they are claiming their birth-rights or fulfilling their destinies.

Because they are so convinced of the truth of this narrative, and because they are so confident and charismatic, some male spiritual teachers are able to convince others that it is true as well. Along the way, they may acquire a flock of followers, assistants, and/or sexual partners—even as they drift ever further from reality.

Thus far I've spoken of alphas solely in psychological and socio-logical terms. But, especially in men, hormones are usually involved as well. Many studies have shown that, among humans, male alpha figures typically have high, or very high, levels of testosterone. Does a surplus of testosterone prod men into becoming alphas? Or does alpha status have a biological effect on men, causing them to produce more testosterone? Or are high testosterone and alpha behavior more a common pairing than a cause and an effect? (High testosterone levels in both men *and* women correlate closely with psychological dominance, high self-esteem, and high confidence.) The jury is still out on this.

We do know, however, that as a man's status in any group rises, so does his testosterone level. (There is some evidence that testos-terone levels rise in female alpha figures as well.) High testosterone levels generally make an alpha male (or any man) more sexually attractive, which creates heightened arousal levels among his fol-lowers. This tends to boost an alpha's testosterone levels further, encouraging him to be more alpha-like—and creating a feedback loop that makes the alpha ever more desirable. This high testos-terone level also makes him very horny—and more likely to do something unwise.

A male spiritual teacher may thus be the center of a swirl of influences, each one perpetuating and boosting the others. The result can be ever higher group status, ever more sexual interest from group members, ever more opportunities to have sex with some of those folks, and ever more hormonal pressure to accept some of these opportunities.

Before we give these teachers too much of our sympathy, however, we might remind ourselves that all of us adults successfully manage our desires, sexual and otherwise, on a regular basis. It's not always easy or pleasant, but it's not impossible, either.

Also, it's not like these circumstances condemn an honorable spiritual teacher to living in a hell realm of unexpressed sexuality. He can, after all, have sex with his partner—or, if he doesn't have a partner, he can find one outside of his spiritual community, or he can masturbate. Unless he comes from a tradition that forbids these options—in which case he and his community may be headed for tragedy.

Yet even if a teacher has no approved option for sexual release, he does have plenty of options for emotional release, which is ultimately more important. He can (and should) talk regularly with a trusted friend or colleague—or his own spiritual teacher, if he has one—about the pressures he feels. In these discussions he should feel free to complain about his students, to privately question or criticize elements of his tradition, and in general to blow off steam. He can also consult with a psychologist, social worker, or member of the clergy from outside his spiritual community.

In any case, wise spiritual teachers know that they are loving, responsible people first and alphas second. Thus they know to ignore or override any impulses that could cause harm. They also know to ignore the voices of their internal false Brahmins, which tell them that they're special, and thus entitled to the sexual delights that some of their students may be happy to provide.

Resistance, good intentions, supportive self-talk, and a strong sense of responsibility will keep most spiritual teachers' sexual boundaries intact in most situations. But during crises, and over the long term, most teachers need at least one caring confidant whom they can call on for help and support, and whom they can talk to in utter confidence. They also need a deep and abiding love for truth, their students, and the Absolute.

Chapter 12

The Sexual Power of Students

IN THE MOST COMMON STORY of sex between a spiritual teacher and their student, the teacher seduces or manipulates the student; the teacher is thus an exploiter, and the student largely a victim. Yet two other scenarios are not uncommon, especially if the teacher is a first-time errant or first-time exceptionalist:

1. The attraction and sexual involvement are mutual from the beginning.
2. The student seduces the teacher.

As we have seen, spiritual teachers can be enormously sexy and—within their spiritual communities—enormously powerful. However, some *students* may also be sexy and powerful, and some will use this power to try to attract, seduce, distract, challenge, and/or test their teachers. This can take a variety of forms, from overt seduction to flirting or teasing. Sometimes these actions are largely unconscious, sometimes quite conscious.

Many different motives can underlie these actions:

- ▶ a desire to share in the teacher's power, insight, and/or status
- ▶ a desire to feel special
- ▶ a desire to couple with a father, mother, or other authority figure
- ▶ a desire to prove or demonstrate the student's own power

▶ a desire to ruin, harm, or control the teacher
▶ a desire for high drama (in which the student may hope to play two sequential roles: first, the trophy partner, then the abused and exploited victim)
▶ a desire to heal old wounds—and/or a compulsion to deepen them
▶ simple, straightforward attraction

As we have seen, not all students who try to seduce their teachers actually want to succeed. Some do it to test their teachers' boundaries, integrity, and authenticity. Like children pushing against their parents' authority, these students hope that their teachers will prove themselves worthy by *not* giving in to pressure.

The human heart being what it is, however, some students will have mixed motives. They may simultaneously want the teacher to resist, thus demonstrating integrity, *and* to succumb, thus giving the student a huge sexual thrill.

To my knowledge, no one has yet conducted a study to determine what percentage of spiritual teachers receive sexual advances from their students. However, psychologist Karen McClintock, author of the books *Healthy Disclosure* and *Preventing Sexual Abuse in Congregations*, estimates that 65–75% of clergy (of both sexes) receive such advances.

All spiritual teachers are of course responsible for maintaining clear sexual boundaries, no matter what a student says or does—even if it means sending or pushing a student away, or running out of the room. But that doesn't mean we students have no responsibilities of our own. We can choose to support or undermine our teachers' wise actions through what we do with our own sexual energy, and how we act in their presence.

Why Spiritual Teachers Should Talk About Sex

As we've seen, it's quite normal for spiritual teachers and their students to be sexually attracted to one another—but acting on this attraction, rather than feeling it fully and letting it go, can cause great suffering.

Too few spiritual teachers talk publicly about this. But I believe they should. They can begin by explaining that such attraction is common and normal; that no one should take these feelings very seriously, either in others or (especially) in themselves; and that these feelings, no matter how intense they may seem at first, typically settle down over time. Teachers might also encourage their students to allow themselves to simply watch these feelings as they wax and wane, without trying to grab on to them, avoid them, or push them away.

This can be especially helpful to new students, and those under age twenty-five, who may have no clue how to live with sexual desires for their teachers without acting on them. They may, for example, tell themselves (and others) that they have been smitten, touched to their cores, etc., by their teacher, and "cannot resist" the teacher's allure. When these folks learn that their desires are common, and even ordinary—and, in fact, no big deal—then those desires may lose much of their power.

Teachers can also speak publicly and matter-of-factly of their own sexual desires. This needn't sound like a confession; it can be simple and straightforward. For example: "In a typical day, I'll encounter lots of people whom I find attractive. Why wouldn't I? I'm human, just like you. But just because I find someone attractive doesn't mean I have to do anything about it. Suppose you walk past a bakery and see a delicious cake in the window. This doesn't mean you have to eat it. You keep walking, and soon you've forgotten about it."

Such frank talk helps students and spiritual communities in multiple ways. It breaks any taboos about discussing the topic; it encourages community members to raise and discuss the subject in the future; and it dispels anxiety. It takes much of the wind out of many students' fears, worries, obsessions, and fantasies. It helps students to see their teachers more realistically. And it promotes greater openness and safety. (Ideally, a recording and/or a transcript of such a talk might be available at no charge on the spiritual community's website.)

At the same time that teachers publicly talk about and discourage teacher-student sexual relationships, they can and should also sing the praises of sex in general, in whatever way is appropriate to their tradition. This double-sided approach is important, because most spiritual communities have some prudes and control freaks. Many of these folks would like to tamp down human sexuality—and would be quick to use their teachers' words in service of these efforts. It might even be wise for teachers to take these community members aside, one at a time, and encourage them to loosen up—and, perhaps, to have more sex.

I hope it's clear by now that I take a similar stand. Let's raise high the flag of seduction, flirting, teasing, and the whole juicy shebang—but let's not wave it in places or ways that will harm people, undermine relationships, or destroy trust.

Chapter 13

Spiritual Insight and Arrogance

THE MOST COMMON ERROR that sincere spiritual teachers make is believing themselves to be wiser or more insightful than they actually are.

Spiritual teachers may or may not be wiser than we are about investing, cooking, repairing cars, finding bargains, dressing fashionably, getting out stains, or backing political candidates. If they *are* in fact wiser on any of these subjects, it's not because of their spiritual training or experience. We're deluded if we think that a spiritual awakening somehow makes our teachers reliable guides on such matters; our teachers are even more deluded than we are if they believe this themselves.

Also, spiritual teachers may or may not have greater psychological or emotional wisdom than we do. It may seem logical—perhaps even obvious—that someone with significant spiritual insight would also be a responsible, mentally healthy adult. But, as we have seen, this simply isn't the case. Spiritual insight and experience are not necessarily indicators of a teacher's personal integration, moral integrity, or mental health. Each of these must be acquired and lived on its own terms. There are no shortcuts, even spiritual ones—and anyone who imagines there are will eventually get into trouble. As Mariana Caplan notes,

[T]here is spiritual growth, and there is psychological development, and we hope that spiritual growth takes care of the psychological development, but it doesn't. What I keep finding are people who have a lot of spiritual wisdom but a lot of psychological blind spots, too.... We bring our own conditioning and psychological being to our spiritual lives, and ideally part of a spiritual path is learning how to make those distinctions, to identify our blind spots, so that we don't get into dangerous situations.

Some spiritual teachers may also judge their own *spiritual* wisdom to be greater than it is. We looked at one cause of this in Chapter 7, in which people assume that a physically or emotionally powerful experience must, by definition, carry great import and bestow great insight. We looked at another cause in Chapter 11, when we examined the tendency of alpha figures—especially male alphas—to see themselves as imbued with special powers or destiny. But several other common factors can also encourage spiritual teachers to have inflated views of their own spiritual insight:

▸ *Teachers' limited contact with people outside of their own spiritual communities.* Because of their roles, spiritual teachers typically spend much of their time working with folks who have less spiritual insight than they do. Over time, through ongoing comparison, it's easy for them to start feeling especially wise. For this reason, it's essential that spiritual teachers regularly spend time out in the larger world, where most people don't give a damn about the teachers' spiritual insight. It's also another reason why spiritual teachers need to talk regularly with their partners, friends, and colleagues—and their own teachers.

▸ *Students' ongoing attention and appreciation.* For some teachers, this also includes students' loving gazes, their swoons, their effusive letters and cards and emails, and/or their gifts of flowers, money, favorite foods, etc. When other people appreciate or adore us, it's easy for us to believe that we deserve their appreciation and adoration—and it's tempting to wallow in them. Wise teachers regularly remind themselves that their role is to serve their students, not be an object of their adoration.

▶ *Students' projections about their teachers' ability and insight.* When everyone around us believes we've got wisdom and skills that we don't, over time we become tempted to believe it, too. Wise teachers need to shake off these projections and routinely tell their students (and themselves), "Here's what I am and here's what I'm not. If you think I'm more than this, you're mistaken."

▶ *The very human desire to feel smart, capable, helpful, valuable, admired, appreciated, needed, indispensable, powerful, in control, and/or in charge.* Wise teachers treat these desires the same way they deal with sexual attraction to their students, or the urge to eat three desserts: they feel those desires fully, let them go, and bring themselves back to love and service.

Any or all of these influences can cause arrogance to slowly creep into a spiritual teacher's heart.

But there are also some spiritual teachers who had arrogant hearts *before* they became teachers. Years ago, they were arrogant (and often charismatic) business leaders, or university administrators, or marketers; then they discovered spirituality, and today they're arrogant and charismatic spiritual teachers. They may have some spiritual insight, but they have not fundamentally changed the way they interact with their fellow human beings.

None of this means that a deeply insightful spiritual teacher can't be strong, assertive, confident, and/or charismatic. (Exhibits A through C: Jesus, Muhammad, and Buddha.) But all of these qualities can meld as readily with humility as they can with arrogance. Furthermore, there is a huge qualitative difference between assertive wisdom and arrogant half-wisdom. It's not hard to smell this difference, though it may sometimes take some weeks or months of sniffing.*

* For readers who want to improve their ability to sniff out arrogance, I recommend once again Mariana Caplan's *Eyes Wide Open: Cultivating Discernment on the Spiritual Path* and *Halfway Up the Mountain: The Error of Premature Claims to Enlightenment*. Caplan is immensely honest and insightful about the ways in which we fool ourselves, and each other, in the name of spirituality. In fact, she has made it her mission to explore and expose the pitfalls of spiritual life, and she does it with great love, wisdom, and eloquence.

Chapter 14

The Spiritual Teacher's Partner: Soulmate or Saboteur?

STUDENTS' PROJECTIONS, judgments, misapprehensions, adulation, and demands for time and attention can all be hard on a teacher. But when teachers have partners or families, those partners and families often face some of the same pressures.

Let's imagine a spiritual teacher named Kim; Kim's partner, Chris; and their recently adopted son Blake, who is six months old. Kim and Chris have lived together for nine years and been married for the last two of these. Kim began teaching ten years ago; Chris has been Kim's student for the past five.

Kim's community and family routinely compete for Kim's time—and students often ask for more time than Kim is willing or able to give. Even though Kim says no when necessary, the situation nevertheless creates tension that requires constant monitoring and management. When Kim leans too far in one direction, Chris feels neglected and resentful. But when Kim leans too far in the other, some students complain that Kim is neglecting them.

Although Chris is on good terms with almost all the community's members, she's bothered by some of the things a few members do. She's seen lots of students put Kim on a pedestal and imagine that Kim is infallible. She's also seen students flirt with Kim; act out in front of Kim; try to monopolize Kim's time and attention; try to make Kim into their surrogate parent; and, on a couple of occasions, try to drive a wedge between Chris and Kim.

Chris also has to deal with the projections that some community members put on *her*. Some seem to think she's Kim's assistant or servant; others imagine she should be Kim's substitute when Kim is out of town. Some think that Chris must be wise because she's Kim's partner; others think that Kim must be wiser than Chris about everything, including where to get a good espresso and what varieties of tomato to grow. Because of all this, Chris sometimes feels frustrated, exasperated, and misunderstood.

Chris and Kim love each other wholeheartedly and want to support each other however they can. But in practice this doesn't always happen. Sometimes Chris feels she competes with Kim's students for Kim's time, attention, and love; meanwhile, some students feel that Chris is selfish, controlling, and not very spiritual. As a result, Chris sometimes acts coldly toward a few of Kim's students—and, on rare occasions, toward Kim.

Unless both partners lovingly address this dilemma together, the situation can easily turn into a vicious cycle. Kim's community and family can become ever more separate worlds—and Kim can be more and more torn between them. If these strains become severe enough, they may eventually encourage Kim to sexually transgress with a community member.

Because this cycle can be so pernicious, it's imperative that Kim and Chris watch for it and consciously work to step out of it. There is no shame in going to a counselor for help with this.

Kim and Chris also need to acknowledge to each other that, by its very nature, their union will always be subject to many more difficulties, stresses, and outright assaults than most partnerships. This means they must be very deliberate about supporting each other during difficult times, and not allowing students to pull them apart.

Kim and Chris must both also acknowledge that there will be times when Kim must make a very difficult choice between Chris and Blake on the one hand, and students or the spiritual community on the other. Yet if Kim and Chris continue to be loving, committed partners, these inevitable choices will not be crazy-making.

It can also be helpful for Kim to talk honestly and publicly about these difficulties. As with discussions of sexuality, these comments needn't be confessional or overly detailed. "As you know, I'm committed to this community, and I'm committed to my family. Most of the time, these commitments run parallel, but once in a while, for an hour or a day or a week, I have to choose one over the other. I wish I could choose both, but sometimes it's simply not possible. Life is full of tough choices, and in the face of them our job is to make the wisest and most loving choice we can, knowing that almost every choice we make will have a down side, and a variety of consequences."

It's also important for Kim and Chris to do all the things other loving, supportive couples do to stay happy and connected. This includes regularly making the time to adore each other, have fun with each other, relax with each other, and make love.

We all need to get away from our spiritual communities once in a while. I therefore strongly recommend that spiritual teachers and their partners blow town together at least twice a year, for at least ten days at a time.

It's also helpful for spiritual teachers and their partners to publicly show their genuine physical affection for each other. This sends a clear message to the spiritual community (and the world) that both partners are committed to each other—not just spiritually and emotionally, but sexually. It also helps to humanize both partners in students' minds.

Since this book is, in part, about how to keep spiritual teachers from losing their way sexually, I also recommend to all hetero spiritual teachers—and all hetero couples—Willard Harley's book *His Needs, Her Needs: Building an Affair-Proof Marriage*. Nothing supports safety in spiritual communities and teacher-student relationships better than a joyous and rock-solid partnership between a spiritual teacher and their partner. For hetero spiritual teachers (and their partners) who are reading this, please consider Harley's book a companion volume.

Chapter 15

The Shadow Side of Celibacy

MANY PEOPLE—including some people on spiritual paths—deeply misunderstand celibacy. They see it primarily as a deliberate withholding of pleasure; or a test of one's will or faith; or a tool for transcending desire, one's body, and/or the world. In essence, they see celibacy as an elevation of the spirit and a denial of the flesh.

All of these approaches to celibacy share a common theme: a focus on the self. Yet healthy celibacy is not about the self at all.

When practiced voluntarily and mindfully, celibacy is an expression of compassion and freedom. It relaxes our grip on the self, and its habitual demands for attention and gratification, and allows us to focus more time and energy on serving other people and the world.

Celibacy frees up enormous amounts of vitality and time that would otherwise be spent on seeking and finding a partner—and, thereafter, on being a lover, a beloved, and, usually, a breadwinner, a parent, an in-law, a grandparent, and so on.

Celibate spiritual teachers thus have the opportunity to redirect this vitality and time toward nurturing the development of their students—and toward service in general.

When spiritual teachers take and maintain a vow of celibacy, they also free their students (and everyone else) from any possibility of sexual entanglement with them—and from the potential frustration, disappointment, fear, clinging, projections, jealousy, etc., that often attend sexual involvement. In essence, teachers recuse themselves from the whole welter of sexual karma—from having kids to getting along with in-laws to quitting their spiritual communities and becoming bankers or electricians in order to support their families. Celibacy thus offers simplicity, serenity, and freedom to spiritual teachers (and other folks) who practice it wholeheartedly.

A spiritual teacher's vow of celibacy also offers safety to their students. It says to students, "You can open your heart to me. You don't need to protect yourself from me, because I promise not to be sexual with you." A kept vow of celibacy thus promotes immense trust between a teacher and their students. (When wholeheartedly kept, a vow of monogamy to a partner also promotes such trust, because it is also a promise to students not to be sexual with them.)

The shadow side of all this is that if the teacher does lose their way, the broken celibacy vow greatly deepens the betrayal and the harm—not just for the student, but for the whole spiritual community.

Healthy and Unhealthy Celibacy

Healthy celibacy is not the renunciation of sexual *desire*, but the renunciation of sexual activity with others. The celibate recognizes that sexual desire is normal and natural, like hunger and thirst. Some traditions thus see masturbation (unless it is compulsive) and orgasm during sleep as natural and appropriate parts of healthy celibacy.

This makes some students uneasy. We have a hard time imagining our beloved teacher masturbating to Miss January or Mr. July. But it's good for us to imagine this. It humanizes the teacher, and makes it harder for us to put (or keep) them on a pedestal.

In contrast, *unhealthy* celibacy seeks to renounce (i.e., repress) sexual desire itself. The problem with this, as any psychology major can tell you, is that trying to forcibly repress any part of ourselves almost never works over the long term. Sooner or later our repressed, shadow side comes roaring back, demanding expression—and it usually gets us, and others, into trouble.

Healthy celibacy, like healthy monogamy, can also be used as an opportunity to fully integrate our sexuality *into* who we are, rather than separate ourselves from it. When spiritual teachers achieve such integration (with or without practicing celibacy), they become stronger, wiser, and less self-centered. But if they split off and repress their sexuality, they can become enormously tempted to transgress. Handling all the pressures described in earlier chapters, plus the pressure of one's own squelched or denied sexuality, can be a literally impossible task, no matter how loving and well-intentioned a teacher might be.

Celibacy is not for everyone—nor should it be. The celibate who can't stop thinking about sex, or who becomes a porn addict or compulsive masturbator, may do themselves a favor by dumping the celibacy (and, if necessary, the role or tradition that requires it of them) and finding a partner.

Celibacy must be entered into voluntarily. Forced celibacy is an almost-perfect setup for sexual misconduct. A teacher who has little appetite for celibacy, but whose tradition demands that they practice it, is ill suited to handling the multiple pressures this book describes. In contrast, a spiritual teacher who willingly vows celibacy, whether or not their tradition requires it of them, is much more likely to maintain that vow with conviction and serenity.

Doubly Forbidden Fruit

As we saw in Chapter 12, some students will try to sexually tempt a teacher in order to test the teacher's authenticity, or to wield and confirm their own sexual power. In the case of a celibate teacher, they may also do it to punish the teacher for being sexually unavailable.

In other instances, some students may feel doubly enticed by the "forbidden fruit" factor. Sex with a celibate teacher is strictly off limits for two reasons: because they're your teacher, and because they're celibate. This makes sex with the teacher a double transgression—and doubly exciting and tempting.

Celibacy generally isn't difficult to maintain when you're a humble monk or nun in a healthy celibate community, where everyone abides by the celibacy rule, dresses modestly, and acts lovingly toward each other. But it is much tougher when you're out in the world with students who dress more or less as they please, some of whom may flirt with you or try to seduce you.

One way we students can respect and support our spiritual teachers is by not acting out sexually in their presence. This is doubly true for celibate teachers. When we tempt or tease them, we make their lives more difficult—and we increase the likelihood that they will lose their way.

Chapter 16

Monogamy and Its Skeptics

IN MOST MODERN CULTURES, monogamy is considered normal and natural—and it is the only widely sanctioned configuration for healthy sexual relationships. Indeed, many anthropologists, psychologists, biologists, and philosophers argue that we humans are designed to be monogamous. Certainly monogamy has provided the foundation for a great many passionate, loving, and stable relationships.

Other folks, however, argue that monogamy is *merely* a cultural and religious norm, not a practice that's hardwired into us. Still others suggest that monogamy is downright pernicious—a way to keep us in thrall to established religions, governments, industries (e.g., the wedding industry), professions (e.g., clinical psychology), and experts (e.g., Dr. Phil).

This debate has raged for a very long time, and it shows no sign of resolving or simmering down. Indeed, as I write this chapter in the summer of 2010, Christopher Ryan and Cacilda Jethá have just reignited and rejuvenated the debate with their fascinating book *Sex at Dawn: The Prehistoric Origins of Modern Sexuality.* Ryan and Jethá make a detailed and eloquent case that evolutionary biologists have largely climbed up the wrong tree. They argue that human sexuality aligns far more closely with that of the polyamorous bonobo (our closest genetic cousin) than with the monogamous gibbon (a much more distant cousin).

Whatever general merits and drawbacks monogamy may have, and however natural or unnatural it may be for us humans, there are nevertheless some good reasons to require noncelibate spiritual teachers to practice it.

In the previous chapter, I explained that when a spiritual teacher practices either monogamy or celibacy, they send a powerful message of safety to their students—a message that says, "You can trust that I will not become sexual with you." A spiritual teacher's monogamy can thus help them to build trust and spiritual intimacy with their students.

I also suggest elsewhere in this book that many spiritual communities would be wise to require their spiritual teachers to be monogamous or celibate. Indeed, I recommend that this expectation often be a part of spiritual teachers' formally defined roles. I suggest this not on ethical grounds, but on practical ones: if a spiritual teacher violates his vow of monogamy or celibacy, a spiritual community's leaders can then require him to step down, not for being immoral, but for failing to fulfill his job description.

Furthermore, for most students, it's tough to build deep trust and spiritual intimacy with a teacher who sleeps around—even if that teacher makes it a point not to sleep with his students. In any event, such an arrangement is quite difficult for any spiritual teacher to maintain. He must draw and hold a clear, firm sexual boundary between himself and his students, while leaving that boundary highly porous for other folks who attract him.

Theoretically, it's possible for a libertine teacher to hold such impeccable sexual boundaries with his students; to jump from bed to bed with other people; to teach with great compassion, insight, and empathy; and to avoid the perils of egotism and self-indulgence over the long term. But I've never encountered such a teacher. I have, however, encountered many monogamous or celibate spiritual teachers who admirably accomplish all of these things except the jumping from bed to bed.

Nevertheless, a common libertine argument goes like this: *Most people are deeply asleep. They don't question the prevailing cul-*

tural, social, or religious norms, and they don't see reality for what it is. As a result, they're easily lied to and manipulated by the media, by politicians, and by other authority figures. Once you enter the stream of spiritual life, however, you begin to wake up from this dream. You start to see how arbitrary, hollow, and stultifying many social conventions really are. As you wake up further, you begin to embrace life in all its beauty and wonder and slipperyness. You live out of your authentic inner essence, grab hold of life, and live it fully and joyously, without regard for the narrow, neurotic limits that our fear-driven culture would impose on you—limits like fashion, manners, and monogamy. So, my brave and compassionate and beautiful protégé, take your clothes off and come here.

That's the version libertines often use with potential suductees. When defending themselves to other folks, libertines typically make a similar pitch, but replace the final sentence with something like this: *I live outside the norms because I see through them. But you're stuck in conventional morality.*

These are stirring speeches—and, except for the last eighteen words of each, there's a lot of truth to them. (This assumes, of course, that the libertine is speaking out of genuine insight, and not just spouting spiritual b.s.) But in those final words, the libertine's speech turns into coercive nonsense.

First, the libertine tends to shamelessly lump monogamy with other, less enduring social norms—in the example above, with fashion and manners—and then to belittle the whole bundle. This is like saying, "Hot fudge sundaes, double cheeseburgers, and communion wafers will all make you fat and unhealthy if you eat enough of them."

Second, there's a world of difference between rejecting monogamy and having sex with one's students. Yet the libertine leaps from the first to the second as if the two were somehow conjoined.

Let's assume for a moment that a libertine teacher and his student live in an imaginary culture where monogamy *is* always a scam and a sham. That would provide excellent cause for rejecting monogamy—but it has *nothing at all* to do with breaking the sexual boundary between spiritual teachers and their students. The teacher might as well say, "Monogamy is dishonest and noxious, so I'm going to have sex with my mother and my kids and my dog."

This is a spiritual shell game. Under the banner of critiquing and criticizing monogamy, libertine teachers sometimes try to write themselves a ticket to do whatever they please. It's a ticket we students would be wise not to honor.

Chapter 17

The Power and Pitfalls of Gurus

THIS CHAPTER LOOKS at a unique form of teacher-student relationship, the guru-disciple relationship, which offers students and teachers singular risks, opportunities, and benefits.

The word *guru* is sometimes used as an informal synonym for "spiritual teacher"—a rough equivalent of *sensei* or *swami* or *sheikh* or *master*. The word is used similarly, but as a formal title, in Hinduism, Jainism, Bön, and Tibetan Buddhism.*

In these four traditions, a guru is considered much more than just a wise and compassionate teacher. In Tibetan Buddhism, for instance, a guru is regarded as a kind of sacred conduit through which the power and blessings of the tradition are transmitted to the student. In other traditions, a guru is a human stand-in for truth or the Absolute, at least from the disciple's viewpoint. Thus the disciple invests in their guru a level of trust, commitment, and spiritual intimacy beyond what they offer to any other human being.

In many cases, the disciple also agrees to be obedient to the guru, based on the mutual understanding that the guru can clearly discern the disciple's spiritual issues and needs—and that the guru will act selflessly and lovingly to support the disciple's spiritual development. As part of this practice, the disciple grants the guru

---

* The title is also used in Sikhism, where it refers to ten specific Sikh spiritual teachers who lived between the fifteenth and eighteenth centuries, as well as to Sikh scriptures.

the opportunity to routinely challenge, prod, and make demands of them. The disciple accepts these challenges, proddings, and demands in the understanding that these will encourage a spiritual opening, and/or a dismantling of the disciple's selfishness and misperceptions. Healthy guru-disciple relationships thus offer disciples the opportunity to go deeper and grow up faster.

These relationships can be particularly valuable in working through our authority issues with the Absolute. Most of us have these issues—big time. A healthy guru-disciple relationship provides an ideal context for confronting and resolving this meta-issue.

A close look at this topic would fill a book of its own, but let me provide one common example. We all want to be treated well—not just by the people we care about, but by strangers, by animals, by businesses, by institutions, by the weather, by circumstances, by our own minds and hearts, and by God. To varying degrees, we also labor under the delusion that, if we do the right things, we can somehow make the world consistently treat us well. The reality, of course—and we know this but may inwardly deny it—is that sometimes things go badly for us no matter what we do. Yet we don't want to accept the profound uncertainty and lack of control that undergird our lives.

Some authentic gurus may help their disciples work through this issue by showering them with love, attention, and kind words one day, then ignoring them—or even publicly dissing them—the next. Typically, the disciple's first response is to try to win back the guru's favor. Over time, however, they may begin to see that life involves more than trying to acquire approval and pleasure—including "spiritual" pleasure—and running away from pain. A wise and loving guru thus does the disciple a great service by helping to engender this realization.

Yet it's easy to see how a deluded or narcissistic guru could use these same tools—praise, attention, ridicule, and rejection—to manipulate their disciples for their own gratification.

In Sickness and in Health

Like other spiritual teachers, gurus' personalities, backgrounds, and lifestyles are widely diverse. Some gurus are celibate, others married or partnered. Some are wise and loving; others are narcissistic, deluded, or exploitive. Some are a mixture of many of these characteristics.

Because of the power granted to the guru, a guru-disciple relationship should *never* be entered into lightly or casually. Indeed, many traditions that support guru-disciple relationships recommend to potential disciples that they careful scrutinize a potential guru over a long period of time—at least several months, and perhaps years—before agreeing to become their disciple. It's also a good idea to talk directly with some of the guru's disciples. Google the guru, too; as a precaution, also Google them plus the word "scandal."

In practice, it's easy for guru-disciple relationships to become dysfunctional. Disciples often project their own parent/child issues onto their gurus, and some gurus overvalue their own insight and/or manipulate their disciples for their own ends.

Yet healthy guru-disciple relationships certainly do occur. I've witnessed some, and they are as sound, sane, and spiritually nourishing as strong marriages. And, like marriages, they should never be entered into without both parties deeply knowing and trusting each other.

In these relationships, as in all healthy teacher-student relationships, both parties typically share the following understandings: the guru is entirely human; the guru can and does make ordinary human mistakes; the disciple does the real spiritual work; the guru's job is to provide guidance—though sometimes in very strong, focused, and, perhaps, emotionally painful form; the disciple is always responsible for their own actions and decisions; and, over time, the disciple is expected—or at least encouraged—to outgrow all dependence on the guru.

Healthy guru-disciple relationships—like all healthy teacher-student relationships—are *always* adult/adult. They are sacred pacts between two sincere and committed human beings with a shared goal: the spiritual opening and deepening of the student.

In contrast, unhealthy guru-disciple relationships that involve a foolish or overly dependent disciple are adult/child, and can be quite painful for the disciple. Those that also involve a narcissistic guru are child/child, and often result in the guru abusing or exploiting the disciple, sexually or otherwise. In such relationships, the disciple finds comfort in abdicating spiritual authority to another human being, while the guru's ego feeds off the disciple's child-like trust and adoration. Tragically, needy disciples and narcissistic gurus have a knack for finding and bonding with each other.

Because of the heightened trust and intimacy inherent in guru-disciple relationships—as well as the exceptionally large power differential between the parties—all of the temptations that spiritual teachers face are multiplied several-fold for gurus. For the same reasons, when gurus do transgress, they can do far more damage to their students than other spiritual teachers—and they tend to go down hard, fast, and in flames.

Chapter 18

Sex as a Spiritual Teaching

SEX CAN OPEN US to truth, to the Absolute, and to each other. It can be sacred and transformative. And it can be a grand opportunity for spiritual learning and healing.

When sex is misused, however, it can keep us from learning. It can sap much of our energy, time, and attention. It can make us more selfish, more foolish, and more deluded. And it can keep us stuck in repetitive behaviors that harm ourselves and others.

Today, some spiritual teachers and writers have made sexuality a cornerstone of their work. Consider, for example, David Deida, author of *The Enlightened Sex Manual*, *Intimate Communion*, *Finding God Through Sex*, and other books that encourage juicy sex, juicier intimacy, more loving partnership, and deepened spiritual insight. Deida regularly leads workshops in sacred sexuality for couples and individuals, in which he offers verbal guidance to help people deepen their love and connection.* Or consider Shmuley Boteach, author of *Kosher Sex*, *The Kosher Sutra*, and other books that encourage similar outcomes, but through the lens of the Talmud and the Old Testament. Or Tim Alan Gardner, whose book *Sacred Sex* offers a somewhat parallel approach for married Christian couples, and who offers seminars on sex, marriage,

---

* Beginning in 2007, Deida became the subject of some controversy, primarily because of his connections to organizations that teach men seduction techniques. He has not, however, been accused of having sex with any of his students.

and spirituality through his organization Marriage Ministries. Or Michael Mirdad, whose book *Sacred Sexuality: A Manual for Living Bliss* offers a very clear and reader-friendly Eastern approach.

Deida, Boteach, Gardner, and Mirdad understand how sex and spirituality can deeply intertwine, and how much we can learn from exploring that unity. Their work, and the work of like-minded spiritual teachers and writers, helps people use their sexuality to become wiser, more loving, and more aware. I applaud such work and hope it will spread to many people, cultures, and religious traditions.

Having sex with one's students and claiming it as a spiritual teaching, however, is an entirely different matter. At best it is a foolish or immature teacher's self-delusion. At worst it is a form of rape. Almost always, it exploits the student for the teacher's own gratification.

We would do well to be deeply suspicious of any teacher's claim that sex with him is a valuable spiritual teaching. For starters, such a claim immediately raises these questions:

▶ Why does he not offer this sex-based teaching to all sufficiently advanced students, regardless of their age, weight, sex, and attractiveness? Why is it, in most cases, that only attractive students are "sufficiently advanced" or "ready" for this teaching? Would it be okay if only very wealthy, very attractive, young white women happened to be "ready" for it? How about only handsome, muscular black men?

▶ Why is sex with the teacher the only possible means of passing on this teaching? Why would all other forms of the teacher's instruction—discussion, meditation, prayer, chanting, movement, study of texts, etc.—be insufficient?

▶ If the teaching genuinely requires the student to have sex, why must the teacher be their sexual partner? Can't the student learn or experience the same thing with their own regular partner, with some advance guidance provided by the teacher?

Crazy-making Choices

There can be a much bigger problem here, however: when a teacher tells one of his students that sex with him constitutes a spiritual teaching, the student is faced with a crazy-making choice. They can be compliant and have sex with the teacher whenever, wherever, and however the teacher wants—and reap the "benefits" of his "teachings." Or they can refuse to have sex with the teacher, and deprive themselves of those supposedly valuable "teachings."

This is paired with an even more disturbing dilemma: are they being exploited or offered a transformative opportunity? Will sex with the teacher help them break through their karma and personal limitations, or only create more of both? Does their urge to say no come from fear and limitation, or from insight and good judgment?

Unless the student is already keen on having sex with the teacher, *either* choice is highly problematic. If they choose sex with their teacher, they lose their autonomy (and, perhaps, their self-respect); if they say no, they not only miss out on the "teaching," but have to live with the knowledge that they may have turned down something spiritually valuable. The more committed the student is to the teacher (or to the tradition, to enlightenment, to the spiritual quest, etc.), and the more valuable or important the "teaching" is purported to be, the more painful the second choice becomes.

This is already pernicious enough—but the teacher may also pressure the student to make the "right" choice, through comments such as these:

- ▶ "Are you committed to the spiritual path or not?"
- ▶ "I see so much potential in you. You have a real chance to go all the way with this practice (or to become enlightened, become my star student or protégé, become a teacher yourself, etc.). Are you going to turn your back on it at this crucial stage?"
- ▶ "You're the only one of my students who is truly ready for this advanced teaching."

▶ "I thought you were serious about this practice, that you had the courage to fully embrace the truth—but maybe I was wrong."

▶ "It's up to you. You can move forward into who you were meant to be, or you can let your ego hold you back."

▶ "You've disappointed me. You've come all this way, and now you're going to give up on yourself (or on the teachings, the Dharma, etc.). Are you going to let your old fears and patterns continue to shackle you?"

▶ "It's the next step in your spiritual development. If you want to stay stuck where you are, then I can't help you."

▶ "Are you going to trust me or betray me? Because if you betray me, you also betray our tradition, our sacred teachings, and your own liberation."

All of these comments deliver the same basic message: *If you don't have sex with me, there's something wrong with you. You're weak, stuck, foolish, uncommitted, fearful, shallow, second-rate, or generally unworthy.*

For the student, these comments up the ante considerably. Now the choice they must make is not just about accepting vs. turning down an important teaching, or taking a step forward vs. standing still. *It is also about choosing spiritual success or spiritual failure.*

This has enormous emotional ramifications for the student, of course. However, their choice may also determine how the student is treated by the teacher, and/or by their spiritual community, in the future. The student may fear—perhaps quite accurately—that if they say no to sex with the teacher, they will be criticized, disdained, ridiculed, removed from the inner circle, or even sent away.

Such comments by a teacher also force the student into a still deeper corner—one the student may not consciously acknowledge or comprehend. *They must now choose between trusting the teacher and trusting themselves.* Furthermore, as they make this choice, their entire relationship with their teacher is on the line. So is their relationship with themselves.

If the student chooses to trust their own heart, head, and gut, they must also acknowledge some extremely difficult and painful truths: that their teacher is sexually acquisitive and manipulative; that he puts his own interests above theirs; that he is not always honest; that the student's trust in him has been at least partly undeserved; and that they now need to consider ending, or at least seriously modifying, their teacher-student relationship. They must also face this final truth: if they've made the wrong choice, it may be the biggest spiritual mistake of their life.

Alternatively, if the student chooses to trust the teacher, they must accept an equally difficult and painful situation. *They can no longer trust their own head, heart, or gut when it contradicts what the teacher says.* They must give up all power of discernment, decision-making, and self-determination. They must give themselves to the teacher, sexually and otherwise, with the complete, childlike trust one would normally place only in God. They also know that if this turns out to be the wrong choice, they are headed for deep and protracted suffering—and, perhaps, long-term sexual and psychological abuse.

Given the way I've framed this dilemma, the wise choice may seem obvious. But when you're part of a community of folks who may have already given themselves away to their spiritual teacher, the wisdom of fleeing may not seem at all clear. For starters, everyone around you may enthusiastically support the teacher; they may also say that in giving yourself to your teacher, you will "at last break loose from the tyranny of your ego" or "finally let go" or "give yourself the greatest blessing imaginable."

With so much on the line, the student is forced to ask themselves this question: *Do I dare to trust myself, when doing so also means no longer trusting my teacher, my community, my friends, and many (or all) of the most important people in my life?* It's a question that students *must* answer on their own—and no one else can answer it for them.

As with so many important spiritual questions, however, the answer becomes clear when we strip out the noise and focus on its essence, which is: *Do I dare to trust myself?* As thousands of years of spiritual wisdom have taught us, the answer to this question is, *yes—and, in fact, you must.* *

---

* I feel obliged to carve out an exception for folks with mental illnesses such as schizophrenia, bipolar disorder, borderline personality disorder, dementia, serious addiction, etc. People with these illnesses often have trouble knowing when to trust their own heads, hearts, and guts and when not to—and they are often wise to doubt themselves. Sadly, this puts them especially at risk for abuse by exploitive spiritual teachers.

Chapter 19

Tantra and Pseudo-Tantra

THE ANCIENT SANSKRIT WORD *tantra* refers to the warp of a loom or the strands of a braid; the root of the word means *to stretch*, or *to continue in an unbroken fashion*. Authentic tantric practices are ancient as well, going back at least seventeen centuries, and, arguably, many more.

Today, tantra continues to be a part of Tibetan Buddhism, Hinduism, Bön, and Jainism; some folks argue that there are tantric influences in Sikhism and Taoism as well.

Here in the West, we also have a kind of secular tantra: people unaffiliated with any religious tradition who call themselves *tantric teachers*. While some of these folks do teach classical tantra, many combine tantric practices with sensory awareness, psychology, energy work, healing, and/or sexual counseling—then package and sell the caboodle as books, videos, workshops, etc. Sometimes these teachers call what they do tantra; sometimes they call it *neo-tantra*. I'll refer to all these secular forms of tantra as *pseudo-tantra*.

I've devoted a chapter of this book to tantra for two reasons. First, in a very small number of tantric teaching lineages, sex between spiritual teachers and their students has been practiced for many generations (and, in rare cases, continues to be practiced today). Within these lineages, teacher-student sex has long been described as both sacred and highly valuable. Second, some teachers of pseudo-tantra may also attempt to have sex with their students, and (despite having broken from all formal religious traditions) may invoke a long tradition of teacher-student sex as a come-on.

In both cases, all my earlier criticisms and cautions regarding teacher-student sex apply. Indeed, given the issues I've noted above, they apply twofold.

A Brief Taste of Tantra

Classical tantra can be quite complex, and involves a variety of forms of meditation, visualization, mantras, and ritual. Although these of course differ from tradition to tradition, tantric practices are considered (at least by tantric teachers and students) to be the quickest and most direct paths to deep spiritual insight.

Unlike what some Westerners believe, classical tantric practices are not a toolkit of techniques for deriving maximum sexual pleasure, more and bigger orgasms, or any type of bigger buzz. Instead, they typically involve (among many other things) transcending or transforming our ordinary self-centered, grasping approach to life and our habitual quest for stimulation and pleasure.

Tantric practices are considered potentially dangerous, precisely because it's quite easy for students to get stuck in—and even addicted to—the various forms of spiritual and physical ecstasy that certain tantric practices generate. Accordingly, many tantric practices are considered advanced, secret, or appropriate only for experienced students.

Tantra is not, as many Westerners imagine, basically about sex. It's about *unity*. In Tibetan Buddhism, for example, many tantric practices involve symbolic or visualized unity with a deity or a buddha. Some (though by no means all) of these practices employ sexual images, which themselves are symbolic of a greater spiritual unity. As Lama Thubten Yeshe explains in his book *Introduction to Tantra: The Transformation of Desire*:

> Tantra provides powerful methods for getting in touch with our essential wholeness. Tantric art is filled with

potent symbols of the unity and completeness characteristic in our fully realized potential. The image of male and
female deities in sexual embrace...is a symbolic portrayal
of the inner unification of our own male and female energies. On a deeper level, their embrace symbolizes the aim
of the very highest tantric practices: generation of a...state
of mind that is supremely suited to penetrate ultimate
reality and free us from delusion and suffering. Thus their
union has nothing whatsoever to with gratification of the
senses but rather indicates a wholly integrated stage....

Many Westerners, for instance, because they have seen
Tibetan paintings and statues showing deities in embrace,
have the mistaken notion that Tibetan Buddhism is
mainly concerned with the sexual contact between men
and women. [But] this is actually representing the experience of total unity—of method and wisdom, bliss and
emptiness—characteristic of the fully enlightened state.

Some tantric traditions, in fact, actually involve *celibacy*: students acknowledge and work with their own sexual energy to
encourage greater spiritual insight. This transformed and transformative sexual energy becomes a gateway to selflessness and/or the
Absolute. When the teacher is wise and the student is open-eyed,
compassionate, and sincere, these practices can be both wholesome
and illuminating.

Pseudo-Tantra

People who teach classical tantra do so as part of a much larger
welter of teachings and practices within their spiritual traditions.
(These folks don't usually call themselves *tantric teachers* or *teachers of tantra*. To them, this would be like Catholic priests calling
themselves *catechism professionals*, or elementary school math
teachers calling themselves *subtraction masters*.) In contrast, teachers of pseudo-tantra often mix traditions together, or sometimes

make no reference to any religious tradition at all (other than to say something like "tantra is an ancient tradition of ecstasy"). Typically, these folks teach "tantric practices" to anyone who is willing to pay for the instruction.

In *Desire: The Tantric Path of Awakening*, Daniel Odier provides a caustic analysis of this motley mix: "[Pseudo-]Tantra in our industrial societies is often an ersatz version in which all the basic principles have been twisted or distorted to fit with our most superficial longings for enjoyment, for orgasm... a confused mix of 1960s therapies and spirituality with a light, Eastern scent."

The pitches for these psuedo-tantric teachings vary widely. Many focus primarily, and quite overtly, on sex, promising "the ecstatically pleasurable power of Tantric Love" or "the best sex ever" or "sexual education, enhancement, healing, and advice."[*] Other pitches speak of sex as a gateway to greater intimacy and love. Still others begin with sex and branch out into emotional healing, self-love, sexual awareness, and other forms of self-help. And some go the whole spiritual distance, emphasizing that tantra is about spiritual transformation, not bigger thrills, and that tantric sex is a vehicle, not a destination.[†]

The variations on these themes are nearly endless. Some teachers of pseudo-tantra lure folks with implied promises of more or better sex, then make a turn toward serious spiritual inquiry. Still others do a double reverse: they use pseudo-spiritual language to sell promises of better sex; then, once people have bitten the hook,

---

[*] I am not suggesting that more pleasurable sex, more and bigger orgasms, etc. are not worth pursuing, or that techniques for achieving them aren't worth learning. But let's not pretend they're profound spiritual practices when our main purpose is to feel—and/or to induce in our partners—a bigger buzz.

[†] As I was completing this book, I received an invitation to attend "Tantra for Erotic Empowerment," a workshop held by two teachers of pseudo-tantra at a sex shop in Minneapolis. Here was the pitch: "Join us for an honest discussion with Mark Michaels and Patricia Johnson, who dispel some of the most popular myths about this ancient tradition. You'll learn how elements of Tantric philosophy and practice can be easily applied to our modern lives in ways that do more than just improve our sex lives."

the teachers instruct their students in spiritual practices that will help them move beyond their grasping and selfishness.

Like all other types of teachers, the folks who teach pseudo-tantra range from talented, wise, and loving to narcissistic and exploitive. Some are trained in classical tantra, some in the fields noted earlier, and some in both. At the far fringes are a few charlatans looking for easy money and easier sex.

Regarding these folks, let me raise two additional cautions: First, teachers of pseudo-tantra are not generally supervised by any spiritual or religious body. This means that if a teacher exploits or abuses a student, no one is likely to defrock him, reign him in, or call him on the carpet (since there is no carpet to call him on) unless he breaks the law. Second, such teachers are rarely part of spiritual communities. Many run their own freelance teaching businesses, working with couples and individuals, and leading group workshops. Many folks who teach pseudo-tantra thus have no community to answer to—and no status as community leaders to lose. Combined with the lack of supervision and authority, this creates an ideal situation for exploiters, who can manipulate their students with few or no consequences.

Thus, though we needn't reflexively avoid teachers of pseudo-tantra, we would be wise to tread quite carefully when looking into them and learning from them.

Chapter 20

Crazy Wisdom and Its Shadow

THE PHRASE *crazy wisdom* usually refers to spiritual guidance or insight that is expressed in seemingly bizarre, counterintuitive, or nonsensical form. Crazy wisdom can appear as words, actions, imagery, or some combination of these. *The left-hand path*, *left-handed tantra*, and *left-handed dharma* are synonymous terms.

Authentic crazy wisdom is more than mere expression, though. It's usually an active call and a challenge. It's a spiritual water balloon thrown at us to help us wake up, open our eyes, change our course, or get out of our heads and back into reality. (An excellent general introduction to crazy wisdom in spiritual and religious contexts is Georg Feuerstein's *Holy Madness: Spirituality, Crazy-Wise Teachers, and Enlightenment.*)

Wes Nisker's sweet and insightful book, *Essential Crazy Wisdom*, defines the term "crazy wisdom" more broadly—as wisdom from any source, spiritual or otherwise, that doesn't make logical sense but nevertheless rings true. Nisker thus sees authentic crazy wisdom in all the major spiritual traditions, in the words of many well-known philosophers, and in the likes of Woody Allen, Lily Tomlin, Groucho Marx, John Cage, Saul Bellow, Joyce Carol Oates, and Stephen Jay Gould. Hats off to him for making these crazily wise choices.

Examples of crazy wisdom abound in the mystical branches of all major religious traditions. However, the term is most often applied to the words and actions of mystics and spiritual teachers in the traditions of Tibetan Buddhism, Zen Buddhism, Advaita (the mystical branch of Hinduism), Sufism (the mystical branch of Islam), and Hasidism and Kabbalism (the mystical branches of Judaism).

Some of the best-known examples of crazy wisdom appear in Sufi writings, particularly the poems of Hafiz and Rumi, as well as in Sufi teaching tales, many of which feature the wise fool Nasruddin. Similar (and, in some cases, nearly identical) crazy-wisdom tales appear in Zen and Hasidism.

One type of crazy wisdom is also exemplified by many Zen koans, which are supralogical stories, dialogues, and questions. Common koans include "What is the sound of one hand clapping?"; "Show me your original face before your parents were born"; and "What is Buddha? Three pounds of flax." Koans often appear impenetrable, but to someone with the appropriate insight, they are actually simple, clear, and obvious. Study of—and meditation on—koans often leads to this insight.

Examples of crazy wisdom appear in nonmystical religious teachings as well. Jesus surely had moments of crazy wisdom, such as when he pushed the moneychangers off the Temple steps. So did Solomon: think of the story from 1 Kings in which he resolved a dispute between two women who both claimed to be the mother of an infant. After some deliberation, Solomon announced, "Bring me my sword. I'll cut the child in half, and each of you can take your share." The liar was happy enough with this solution, but the child's real mother immediately shouted, "Please, my Lord, give her the child—do not kill him!" Solomon, who of course had no plan to kill the baby, then knew who the real mother was, and granted her custody of the child.

A parallel story exists in Buddhism. In a ninth-century Chinese monastery, some monks were arguing over who owned a cat. Zen teacher Nanchuan took the cat, held it up before all the monks, and announced, "Unless you can say a word of Zen, I will cut this cat in half!"

According to the story, no one moved or spoke. None of the monks walked up to Nanchuan, took the cat, and carried it outside—thus "speaking a word of Zen" through mindful, appropriate action. Nor did anyone shout, "Yo, Nanchuan! Put down the frickin' cat!" In every version of this story I have encountered, Nanchuan then slices the cat in half, killing it. (If we make the dodgy assumption that all parts of this tale are literally true, then in killing the cat Nanchuan may have strayed from crazy wisdom into ordinary craziness.)

Examples of crazy wisdom also appear with surprising frequency in our everyday lives; we often use the phrase "crazy like a fox" to acknowledge such an act. Indeed, many of us routinely use crazy wisdom, sometimes without realizing it. Consider these two common examples:

1. Your eight-year-old daughter expresses an interest in smoking cigarettes when she gets older, so you say "Cool!" and buy her a pack of unfiltered butts. Then you stand by with a bottle of water as she lights up, takes a deep drag, and doubles over in a coughing fit.

2. A mediator watches two disputing people come very close to agreement. Then, on the verge of settling the matter, both dig in their heels for hours over a final trivial point. The mediator throws up her hands and announces with (feigned) exasperation, "I see no hope of any agreement here. Both of you should stop wasting your time. Go home, hire lawyers, and plan on spending the next year in court." She gathers up her things and hurries out of the room—after which the two surprised people look at each other and say, "What's her problem? We're not that far apart. Let's finish this deal." And they do.

Authentic crazy wisdom provokes us to see in a new way, to blast out of a mental or emotional rut, to make an intuitive leap, to connect to a deeper part of ourselves, to move beyond our fears, or to act from direct perception instead of thought. Wielded appropriately by wise teachers, crazy wisdom can thus be an enormously helpful teaching tool.

Wisdom First, Craziness Second

Authentic crazy wisdom is not rational, at least on the surface—but it is often suprarational. An act or utterance of crazy wisdom may be carefully considered, planned, and executed—or it may be spontaneous and intuitive. In some cases, it can be helpfully explained or analyzed after the fact. In other cases, however, it cannot: it was simply the right thing to do at the time. The forms that crazy wisdom can take are thus as diverse as humanity itself.

In the hands of a spiritual teacher, however, *all* acts of authentic crazy wisdom share an essential commonality: *They serve the student, not the teacher.* In this way they replicate other, more rational flavors of wisdom.

Authentic crazy wisdom is wholesome, not dangerous. What *is* spiritually dangerous is students' inability to tell crazy wisdom from simple craziness. More dangerous still is when a narcissistic or immature spiritual teacher confuses the two—or is willing to exploit a student's confusion of them.

Unfortunately, many innocent students have neither the insight nor the experience to distinguish genuine crazy wisdom from ignorance, delusion, neurosis, intoxication, exploitation, narcissism, abuse, or mental illness—or, for that matter, a teacher's simple lack of skill. If a spiritual teacher does anything illogical or weird, these students may automatically interpret it as a manifestation of crazy wisdom—and, thus, as a profound spiritual teaching. Indeed, if the teacher's behavior *doesn't* make sense—or doesn't follow the norms of their religious tradition or culture—then, the student naïvely concludes, it *must* be a very wise teaching indeed. Even if it appears transparently outrageous and exploitive to everyone else (or, at least, to everyone outside the teacher's spiritual community), the student believes it must be wholesome and valuable in some transcendent manner that they don't yet understand, but hope to some day.

It's not hard to see what a steep and slippery slope this can quickly become. The student ultimately becomes willing to accept anything and everything their teacher dishes out, without question or complaint, no matter how seemingly illogical or unwholesome, precisely *because* it is seemingly illogical or unwholesome, so long as the teacher declares (or implies) that it's crazy wisdom.

This can especially be a problem for students who are attracted to crazy wisdom primarily for its craziness rather than its wisdom. These folks admire and gravitate toward weirdness, contrarianism, and/or rebellion wherever they find it, whether or not it is wise or justified. The shadow side of this knee-jerk distrust of whatever is normal or socially acceptable is a naïve acceptance of anything contrary to those norms. As a result, these students can become exploiters' most compliant victims. In essence, such a student says to the teacher, "If you're a exploiter, I'll be your victim."

Crazy wisdom thus becomes the perfect excuse, explanation, and scam. It can be used to justify absolutely anything, and the student cannot argue with it or challenge it on any comprehensible terms. "He was drunk," "She was having a bad day," "He made a mistake," "He put his own interests before mine"—these and all our other usual ways of understanding human behavior get swept off the table and become replaced with a single, one-size-fits-all paradigm: "It was crazy wisdom."

Genuinely wise spiritual teachers will have none of this, of course, and will refuse to exploit their students in any way. But a spiritual teacher with limited insight and exploitive tendencies may have no qualms about manipulating naïve and vulnerable students and declaring his own actions to be crazy wisdom.

In such cases, the student is forced into one of two options: accept everything the teacher does, no matter how outrageous, as a valid spiritual teaching, or doubt the teacher's motives, reject his legitimacy as a teacher, and get the hell away. The first choice means relinquishing their own power to analyze, evaluate, test, question, or discern. It may also mean becoming the teacher's puppet. The second option means losing many or all of their most important relationships; admitting to themselves and others that they've made an enormous mistake; and, perhaps, rebuilding their life from the ground up.

All Craziness, No Wisdom

When crazy wisdom is used as a scam or excuse by unscrupulous teachers, it can take any of three general forms. In the first, teachers claim outright that some or all of their actions are crazy wisdom. In the second, they make no such claim, but publicly sing the praises of crazy wisdom, behave badly, and refuse to explain their actions—thus encouraging their students to connect the dots and infer that crazy wisdom is behind (and justifies) their misdeeds. In the third, teachers delude *themselves* into believing that a universal wisdom is acting through them, and that they can therefore do whatever they please, because that wisdom is running the show. They thus give up *their own* power to analyze, evaluate, test, or discern—and become puppets of their own impulses and desires. This delusion can be especially harmful to both teachers and their students.

All crazy-wisdom scams are crazy-making to some degree. But when a teacher uses the crazy-wisdom dodge to lure a student into bed, this is his essential message: *You should have sex with me. You might not want to, and you might feel it's a bad idea, but you're wrong. It's good for you. It may look like exploitation or manipulation or abuse, but it's not. I can see this, but you can't, because I'm wise and you're not, and I'm acting from a more spiritual orientation than you are. You need to trust me on this.* If the teacher also accuses a reluctant student of a lack of trust, loyalty, commitment, or courage, the situation becomes more crazy-making still. And if the teacher presents the student with a stark choice between obedience or banishment—or says, "If you ever expect to learn anything from me, you must never question me or my actions"—then he's committing serious abuse.

Crazy Wisdom's Bottom Line

We all need authentic crazy wisdom in our lives, and at times we need to use it to serve others.

Crazy wisdom can promote and encourage profound love, growth, insight, letting go, and long, deep belly-laughs.

Authentic crazy wisdom can be used lovingly by spiritual teachers to serve their students. Genuine crazy wisdom can also involve sex (as it can anything else). But there is no valid reason why crazy wisdom needs to involve sex between a spiritual teacher and their student.

If a spiritual teacher tries to have sex with you, and uses crazy wisdom as part of their pickup line, doubt the wisdom but not the craziness—and get away quickly.

As Tibetan Buddhist teacher Sangye Drolma points out, "You have to use the same moral standards for an enlightened person as you do for a normal person. Enlightenment is no justification for sociopathic [or other harmful] behavior." Zen teacher Norman Fischer goes further: "Some might say that the higher degree of enlightenment [one has], the more flexibility one has to use rule breaking as teaching, but I would say the opposite. The more you are serving as an example to the community, the more it behooves you to practice stronger ethical conduct as an example....Nobody is awakened enough to be hurting people 'for their own good.'"

One final note: crazy wisdom is just one form of wisdom. Let's not forget that sane wisdom—and even boring, rational wisdom—can also have great value.

Chapter 21

How Exploiters Crash and Burn

THE SLOPE to exploitiveness is not always steep, but it can be very slippery indeed.

Once a teacher falls (or leaps) into exploitiveness, it's very costly for him to get out. If he admits his transgressions, he may lose his job, his reputation, his spiritual community, and the love and respect of its members—and, very likely, access to sex with his students. If his transgression is serious enough, he might also be defrocked, sued, and/or charged with a crime.

Faced with the choice between more sex, admiration, and gratitude from students on the one hand, and an imagined future as a Walmart greeter or prison inmate on the other, few exploiters will take a deep breath and do the right thing. Most will try to keep a lid on the situation. This of course only ups the ante, making the teacher's inevitable fall harder and more painful for everyone.

Unless the exploiter is a very forthright libertine, none of his misconduct can take place without silence and secrecy—and, as columnist Regina Brett has sagely noted, "If a relationship has to be secret, you shouldn't be in it."

Sometimes the teacher's sexual partner(s) will be as eager to keep things quiet as he is. Often, however, he may try to coax a pledge from them. Some common tactics: "Don't tell others in the community. They wouldn't understand." "If people find out, they'll be jealous of you, and of the special bond we have, and they'll punish you for it." "The other students aren't advanced enough to see what's really going on with us." "Some people in the community have their own agenda. They'd love to get rid of me. If they found out about us, they'd force me out. You don't want that to happen, do you?" This is the same language used by child abusers and other perps to keep their victims quiet.

Sometimes threats replace coaxing: "Don't tell a soul. If you do, I'll have you banished from the community." "Remember, this is a secret teaching. Tell anyone and you destroy its power—and your opportunity for further spiritual advancement." "You're so close to breaking through. But if you want to throw it all away and start again with a lesser teacher, that's your business."

This secrecy often evolves into the teacher—and usually the student as well—living double lives. The two may also begin lying to their families and/or to members of their spiritual community.

Inevitably, though, the exploiter's web begins to fray. This may take days, weeks, months, or even years. It sometimes begins when a community member witnesses—or finds evidence of—one of the teacher's sexual encounters. In other cases, the student begins to feel exploited rather than special. If the teacher has had multiple partners, his web can start to fall apart when one partner confides in another and learns of other liaisons. ("The bastard! He told me I was the only one, too!") The unraveling can also begin when a community member who has known of and tolerated the teacher's misconduct for some time can no longer abide it.

At this point the teacher's most honorable option is to end his sexually exploitive behavior; tell the full truth, publicly admitting to his own weakness and failure; make an appropriate public apology; face the possible shock, horror, and outrage of community members; and honorably accept the consequences, which will likely include dismissal and, perhaps, the end of his teaching career.

Some teachers do wake up and face the music at this point. But those who don't may spin more (and more convoluted) webs. Here are some common examples:

► The teacher admits to the sexual encounter(s), but insists that there is nothing wrong with them, for one or more of the reasons discussed in Chapter 3. ("After all these years, you still think I have ordinary selfish motives. Have you been paying attention to *anything* I teach?")

► The teacher refuses to discuss the issue and tries to rally supporters around him, often with appeals to loyalty. ("I'm your teacher. If you're going to question what I do, you're clearly not ready for what I teach. You can either trust me and my teachings, or you can find another teacher. There are plenty of others out there.")

► The teacher tries to deflect the issue back on his challengers. ("This practice isn't about blaming others. It's about purifying your own mind. Look at yourself instead. Why do you have this desperate need to blame me?")

► The teacher claims that each accuser is lying, mentally ill, and/or out to get him. ("She's been seeing a psychotherapist for nine years. Most of you have seen her crying in public. I'm sorry to have to say this in front of the whole community, but the poor woman's seriously unbalanced.")

The first three of these self-protective strategies share the same essential message: *You're the one with the problem, not me.* The fourth uses the oldest trick in the exploitation playbook: blame the victim.

All of these strategies force each member of the spiritual community to take a stand for or against the teacher. Some fall in line behind him, becoming his personal protection force and blaming his victim(s); others turn into inquisitors and pressure him for the truth. Public meetings may begin to resemble legal hearings.

Throughout this process, community members typically go through a wide range of reactions, which can include confusion, disbelief, shock, horror, denial, grief, outrage, bitterness, helplessness, and/or righteous indignation. Many feel betrayed. Some blame themselves. ("It's our fault. We saw it all happening and kept silent." "How could we not see it? It was right in front of us. Were we blind?" "I should have spoken up the first time I saw the two of them holding hands." "What a fool I've been all these years, falling for all his spiritual bullshit.") Others blame community leaders or inner-circle members. ("They knew about this and didn't say a word! They're as guilty as he is.")

Some community members will feel disoriented or set adrift. In close-knit spiritual communities, where people may have given up jobs, severed family ties, or surrendered financial assets in order to join, students may feel forced to reconsider everything about their lives—or to rebuild them largely from scratch.

They may also feel caught between two worlds: the world of their teacher and community, whom they no longer trust, and the larger world, which includes their families of origin. If, in the larger world, they have loving and empathetic people they can turn to, those folks can help them heal and move forward. If they don't, however, they may be forced to choose between painful isolation and further emotional wounding from relatives or friends who have their own strong beliefs and agendas:

▶ "We told you so. It's your own damn fault for joining a cult. Whoever even heard of Sufism, anyway?"

▶ "You can still make things right. Repent, get baptized, and pray for forgiveness."

▶ "So you've finally woken up and realized that religion is a crock of crap and spirituality is a fantasy for weaklings."

▶ "We've signed you up for eight weeks of deprogramming, followed by twice-weekly psychoanalysis with Dr. Himmelfarb. You'll like him. Your mother and I have been seeing him for the last twenty-five years."

Meanwhile, throughout all this, the exploiter's victims may be ignored or pushed aside as the community focuses on the teacher, his guilt or innocence, and what to do with him. Some of the essential features of spiritual community—safety, respect, compassion, and mutuality—may get washed away. This is when the teacher's victims most need the support of their spiritual community; if they do not receive this support, they may feel victimized a second time.

At some point—especially if the teacher persists in his defensive tactics—the exploiter's victims may bring in a lawyer. Fearing that the organization may be legally responsible for the exploiter's actions, and thus liable for hundreds of thousands of dollars in damages, leaders of the spiritual community may then get their own lawyer. At this lawyer's urging, the entire situation may then become viewed through the lens of potential legal liability. Everything shifts. Public meetings may cease; discussions become private and confidential. Communication to the larger community may shrink to a trickle of vague updates. ("The process of working through this issue continues. Our legal counsel has urged us not to release any details at this time.") Once this happens, lawyers rule the process. Unless leaders act mindfully to maintain a sense of community, members can feel like largely powerless onlookers.

While many different outcomes are possible from here on, they all share two central features: the spiritual community has been deeply wounded, and the trust and respect of its members have been deeply fractured.

Chapter 22

How Errants and Exceptionalists Fall (and Sometimes Rise Anew)

By DEFINITION, errant teachers don't exploit, manipulate, or otherwise harm their students. Instead, over time, an errant teacher falls for one of his students—and the student simultaneously falls for him. The same is true of well-intentioned exceptionalists, who may be guilty of ignorance and naïveté, but not of exploitation or (in most cases) self-deception.

Here is one view of how and why such relationships often begin:

> But there are also some good reasons spiritual teachers seem to end up in the sack with their students so often. Those of us who teach this so-called spiritual stuff are deeply interested in it. Lots of us have invested our whole lives in it. It's really hard to find someone else who shares that kind of real passion for self-exploration, and when you meet someone who does it's almost always a student.

True enough. If you're looking for people who have serious spiritual inclinations that align with your own, of course the place you'll likely find them is in your own spiritual community. But if you're a teacher of that community, the more important issue is how to deal with this dynamic. Some teachers and traditions say that this is precisely why spiritual teachers should be celibate—though, as we have seen, this can create its own issues and problems. Other teachers—and many clergy and mental health professionals—cite this dynamic as a key reason why sexual relationships between spiritual teachers and their students should be outright prohibited. There is some wisdom in this position; however, as I discussed in Chapter 1, it's possible to be just as wise but less hard-edged about the issue.

Wise and Unwise Choices

An errant or exceptionalist who has broken a vow of celibacy has harmed his spiritual community; one who has broken a vow of fidelity to his partner has harmed his partner as well. But what about teachers who are otherwise unpartnered, and who have not taken vows of celibacy? When such a teacher and his student fall for each other, and the two treat each other as equals, how much harm is actually done to anyone?

In many cases, not much—if both the teacher and the student act quickly and mindfully.

Since the essential problem in such a relationship is the teacher's dual teacher/lover role, one part of that role usually has to go. One option is for the two to quickly end the romance and, equally quickly, go public about it. The teacher can then simply apologize and take his lumps like a grownup. Since the attraction was mutual, and since there was no exploitation, manipulation, secrecy, or deceit, those lumps may turn out to be small.

A second option is for the teacher and student to continue their romance but end their teacher-student relationship. For this to work, however, they must very publicly announce both their romance and the end of their teacher-student relationship as quickly as possible. Then, in the weeks and months that follow, it must be clear to the community that their teacher-student relationship is indeed over—

i.e., that their student-teacher "divorce" is real. The student might formally align themselves with another teacher, or might actively go looking for one. At minimum, it typically means that that the student no longer attends the teacher's talks, workshops, retreats, classes, and other such activities (though they might show up at community social events).

The teacher also has a third option: to choose the romantic relationship over his community role as a spiritual teacher. There is much that is honorable in this—and there is plenty of precedent for it. Outside of spiritual communities, lots of people choose love over career. Think of all the folks who quit their jobs and follow their partners to new professions, cities, countries, and lives.

Imagine a spiritual teacher making this statement to his spiritual community: "I'd like to publicly announce that Lee and I have become a couple. We've been growing closer for some time, and a few days ago we declared our love for each other. We've also agreed that our relationship is more important to us than my role as teacher. So, effective ten days from today, I'm stepping down from my teaching role, and Lee has begun looking for a new teacher. A few days ago, I informed the governing board of our decision, and they've accepted my resignation. I look forward to remaining part of the community, and have volunteered to help the board look for a new teacher." Some jaws would drop. Community members would feel confusion and dismay for a time. Some prudes and prigs might briefly kick up a fuss. But there has been no dishonesty, secrecy, or exploitation. Furthermore, the teacher and student haven't run off together or put themselves in opposition to the community; instead, they've renewed their commitment to it in an important way. In the end, little or no harm would be done. (Some students may feel abandoned, and this may stir up a different set of problems—but it's not the result of any wrongdoing.) The shakeup might even initiate a period of community renewal. It's also possible that, after a time—perhaps a year or two—the community might ask the teacher to take his old job back.

For either the second or third scenario to work out, however, both teacher and student must be genuine equals in their romance—i.e., it must not involve any power dynamics that significantly favor the teacher. If the teacher is in fact sexually exploiting the student and fooling himself about his own motives, the couple has no healthy future together.

And in all three of these scenarios, it's essential that the teacher go public about the romance very soon after he and his student declare their love for each other—and before they get seriously sexual. The longer he waits to go public, and the more sexual they get before he does, the more his delay becomes a form of secrecy.

In real life, sadly, the third scenario I've described is quite rare. I'm not aware of *any* spiritual teacher who, when faced with a choice between a romantic relationship and his teaching role, has chosen the relationship. Here are the far more common scenarios:

▶ *The teacher and student go public about their dual relationship and refuse to give it up; the teacher also refuses to give up his teaching role.* This transparency honors the community and may keep problems from multiplying. However, the teacher's attempt to have things both ways may nevertheless throw the community into havoc, or even tear it apart.

▶ *The teacher ends the romantic relationship, but tries to keep it a secret and continue on as if the romance hadn't occurred.* This almost never works; eventually word gets out, and community members may be outraged—by the romance, the secrecy, or both.

▶ *The teacher tries to maintain both the relationship and his teaching role by keeping the relationship secret.* Once a teacher makes this choice, he's slipped into the realm of exploitation. Many more exploitive behaviors then tend to follow: coaxing his sexual partner into silence, misleading his other students, and, eventually, living a double life. From here it's often a fast, steep spiral downward.

In short, when a spiritual teacher and their student fall in love—and treat each other as romantic equals—there needn't be a scandal. Once secrecy enters the picture, however, a scandal becomes almost inevitable.

Chapter 23

Disillusion and Dissolution

A SPIRITUAL TEACHER'S FALL—or flaming crash—can injure or even kill a spiritual community. Sometimes, too, it can do immense damage to its members. But it can also wake people up, help them grow out of their immature notions of spirituality, and encourage them to renew their commitment to their fellow human beings, truth, and serious spiritual inquiry. It can also instigate some valuable community-wide reflection, redesign, or renewal—and, perhaps, a recommitment to the community's core principles and values.

In this chapter we'll look very briefly at the most common scenarios that follow a spiritual teacher's fall. These are not mutually exclusive; indeed, most spiritual communities in crisis go through two or more of them—often in sequence, but sometimes simultaneously. All involve a good deal of pain, but not all of them end badly.

Further transgressions come to light. More victims and witnesses may come forward with stories or accusations. Often these involve additional sexual transgressions; sometimes they involve other forms of exploitation, abuse, or manipulation. Occasionally they involve financial misconduct. Sometimes other leaders, or an entire inner circle, may be implicated along with the teacher.

The community suffers a schism. Some students rally around the wayward teacher, fervently defending him; others demand that he be punished and/or ousted. The teacher and his loyalists may lash out at those who oppose him, accusing them of disloyalty, heresy, or sin. He may punish them or even try to banish them. Community members feel forced into picking one side or the other. A power struggle ensues. Eventually, some people (perhaps including the teacher, or all those who oppose him) are forced out. Others leave in frustration or disgust. Some break away and start something new; others leave and look for a replacement teacher.

The community dissolves temporarily into havoc. In the healthiest version of this scenario, this provides a huge opportunity for positive change. New leaders emerge who spearhead a process of intense organizational self-examination. Community members review the organization's mission, structure, policies, finances, leadership, and spiritual practices. Everything gets questioned and publicly reevaluated. People listen to each other, and everyone gets to speak. This is all very hard work, and it typically takes many months, possibly several years. But slowly, over time, a new and far more functional organization emerges.

In one common but less healthy version of this dissolution, a new (and sometimes charismatic) teacher emerges, or is recruited from outside the community, and takes the old teacher's place. However, the fundamental dynamics of the community remain unchanged, and more havoc and suffering eventually follow. In another common variation, the community falls apart entirely, and its organizational structure stops operating. In the least healthy scenario, the teacher maintains his role and consolidates his power; a reconfigured community coalesces around him. Usually this community is smaller, less healthy, and more cult-like.

Some people suffer personal crises of faith, doubting not only the teacher, but their spiritual tradition—or, perhaps, all spiritual traditions. In bitterness and disgust, some find a new tradition or sect; others swear off religion in general. But some discover that they have learned a great deal—and, paradoxically, that their faith has deepened. Still others see how their own misconceptions or expectations about their teacher—or their spiritual community, or truth—have gotten in their way. As a result, they may feel relieved, renewed, and free, as if they have awakened from a bad dream.

Some people see the crisis as an opportunity for serious personal self-reflection. These folks ask themselves many honest and penetrating questions: What were their motives for studying with the teacher? Which aspects of their relationship with the teacher were healthy, and which were unhealthy? What motives and desires have undergirded their own spiritual quest? Which of these are loving and healthy, and which ones may not be? What would be wise for them to do differently in the future? What is their next step?

The teacher's family comes apart. The teacher's partner may divorce him, or separate from him temporarily. The partner may insist on couple's counseling—or on counseling just for him.

Some community members' families come apart as well— especially those of the students with whom the teacher had sexual liaisons. If the community suffers a schism, some families and couples may be pulled apart when people take competing sides. Relationships can also end when some folks stay in the community and others leave it.

Other families, however, may become closer, more stable, more loving, and more awake as the community descends into havoc— especially if the community later comes back together in a stronger, saner form.

The teacher leaves (or flees, or is forced out of) the community. In some cases, he may establish, or be hired by, another spiritual community—in which case he may create similar situations elsewhere. However, the teacher may also see the wisdom of abandoning his role as a spiritual teacher, at least for a time. Instead, he may follow one of the scenarios I suggested in Chapter 1, becoming a full-time writer or speaker on spiritual topics. He may even excel in such a role, through which he can offer the best of himself to the world without having to face the temptations that created so much trouble for him and his spiritual community.

Dissolution often follows disillusionment: as some members of a spiritual community leave it, the organization may begin to dissolve (or implode). But what looks like the imminent death of a spiritual community may turn out to be the first stage of its strengthening and renewal. As Nancy Myer Hopkins observes in *The Congregational Response to Clergy Betrayals of Trust*, "A crisis can have the effect of breaking open a congregation.... If people will work hard to respectfully listen to one another, to avoid laying blame, to stay the course and to work through the pain together, a much stronger congregation can emerge."

Disillusionment is always painful—but it can be deeply valuable as well. Disillusionment is, after all, our growing out of illusion and into reality—i.e., how things are versus how we wish or imagine them to be. To a large degree, becoming disillusioned equals growing up.

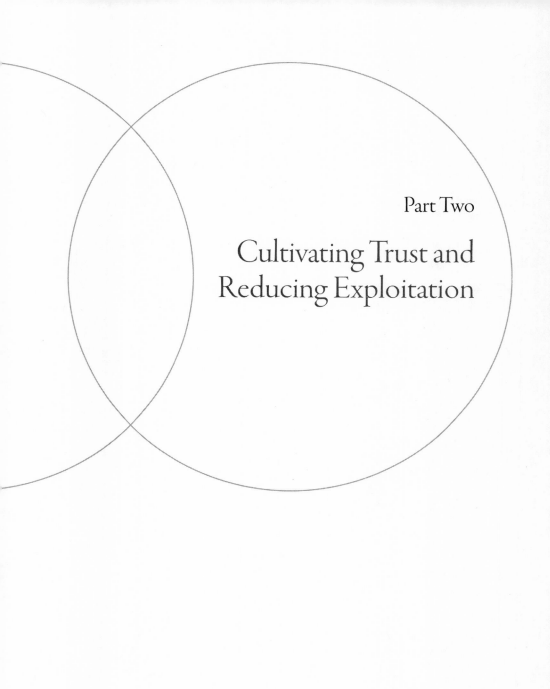

Part Two

Cultivating Trust and Reducing Exploitation

Chapter 24

Spiritual Community and Sexual Transgression

THUS FAR, we've looked at what we students can do, person by person and breath by breath, to support our spiritual teachers' emotional and spiritual health. Now let's consider what we can do as members of spiritual communities and other groups.

As insight meditation teacher Jack Kornfield notes, "The problems of teachers cannot be easily separated from the communities around them. A spiritual community will reflect the values and behavior of its teachers and will participate in the problems as well. Because spiritual community is so important, only when our community life is made a conscious part of our practice can our own heart and spiritual life become integrated and whole."

The healthier a spiritual community is, the more it supports its teacher's wholesome conduct. But what does a healthy spiritual community look like? I propose the following description:

> Members of a healthy spiritual community—including its teacher(s)—are honest, transparent, loving, and supportive of each other. They also have some more specific obligations: to speak up whenever an ethical or professional boundary appears to have been crossed; to refuse to keep secrets, even when asked to do so by teachers,

community leaders, and/or board members; and, in the event of a conflict, to be loyal not to the teacher, or to any particular community member, but to the truth, and to the long-term safety of community members.

The Middle Path of Support

Teachers can only teach us if we allow them to. No matter how much power they may wield, ultimately they teach at our discretion. In groups, we students always have the power to turn them out; as individuals, we always have the power to turn away.

This makes teachers' actions, decisions, and speech partly the responsibility of their spiritual community. If a teacher does something harmful and we students don't say or do anything about it, we become enablers, encouraging our teacher to do further harm.

We students must walk a narrow middle path between the twin cliffs of micromanagement and indifference. It's not an easy path to walk. If we oversee our teachers too closely, we become like overbearing mothers; if we pay too little attention, we give them less than adequate support.

One of the many reasons why some spiritual teachers lose their way is because they can—that is, because no one in their spiritual communities stops them or challenges them. This passive acceptance of misconduct is a form of collusion, and it does immense harm to everyone involved.

Our responsibility as students is complicated by the fact that spiritual teachers' private lives are not as private as most other people's. Because of their unique roles, what they do off duty in public should be legitimately subject to scrutiny, just as with judges, police officers, and ordinary clergy. "Spiritual teacher" is not a mere 9-to-5 job; it is a way of being in the world. The way spiritual teachers treat their kids, neighbors, and car mechanics matters to us.

This doesn't mean that spiritual teachers should have no private lives at all. Like the rest of us, they shouldn't be monitored in their own homes (except when we are their guests), and we shouldn't set limits on what they are allowed to think or feel. We muck up their lives if we become voyeurs, nosenheimers, or gossips.

Secrecy, Privacy, and Disclosure

Loyalty can be a great virtue. It can also be terribly damaging. Mindless loyalty to a teacher who loses his way—even when that loyalty springs from genuine gratitude—ultimately serves no one, and usually makes problems worse.

When news of a spiritual teacher's misconduct makes its way to community leaders, what happens next says a great deal about the health of that community. In a healthy community, leaders promptly look into the misconduct—and, if the accusations seem credible to them, they quickly make those accusations public. They understand that disclosure reduces future harm; that community members have a right—and a need—to know what happened; and that, in the absence of real information, rumors and speculation will quickly spread to fill the vacuum.

In an *unhealthy* community, leaders may circle the wagons and try to keep a lid on the information, in the futile hope of protecting the teacher—or, worse, in the equally futile (and foolhardy) hope of protecting the community from itself. In extreme cases, community leaders may also punish or ostracize anyone who dares to go public with the truth. In such a case, the community behaves very much like an incestuous family.

But experience teaches us that attempts to maintain institutional secrecy ultimately fail. Eventually some community member speaks up. And once news does leak out, the past secrecy is guaranteed to multiply the damage done to community members.

There is an essential qualitative difference between privacy and secrecy. Privacy creates or supports safety; secrecy undermines it. In deciding whether to reveal or withhold information, community leaders need to ask themselves, *Will this create or undermine the safety of community members?*

Difficult as it may be for everyone, a clear and complete description of a spiritual teacher's misconduct (or their credibly alleged misconduct) needs to be promptly made public, to both the spiritual community and the world at large. Though it may feel otherwise at the time, this public sharing of information is the first step of healing. As Marie Fortune notes in *Is Nothing Sacred?*, "...we should never underestimate the power of the explicit acknowledgment of violation in the process of healing for victims. Simple though it is, verbal acknowledgment conveys a depth of understanding and compassion that cannot be accomplished in any other way."

In sharing this information, leaders need to be mindfully and scrupulously honest. They must be very clear about what is known; how it became known; what isn't yet known; and what will happen next. They also need to carefully avoid interpreting information or connecting dots.

Perhaps the most difficult part of this disclosure involves revealing the names of the people with whom the teacher has admittedly or ostensibly transgressed. This can be quite painful for the students who get named, and for their families, but it is deeply important to the healing process.[*]

In some cases, these students may request silence or anonymity out of fear, or shame, or a concern that they will be violated a second time (e.g., blamed or vilified or ostracized). This concern is often well justified: in an unhealthy spiritual community, any or all of these things may happen. It's important for community leaders to protect and support these students as best they can. At the same time, however, leaders must not keep secrets, for these will undermine the health of the entire community. It's a difficult balancing act, and it requires as much mindfulness and compassion as leaders can muster.

How and when this information is revealed says a good deal about

---

[*] There are some exceptions—most notably when minors are involved. Indeed, in some cases, the names of these people *must* be kept confidential by law. In the state where I live, for example, this would be the case if a teacher was found guilty of criminal sexual conduct and his victim was under eighteen—or if his victim formally requested anonymity.

the health of a spiritual community and the wisdom of its leaders. The information needs to be disclosed compassionately, respectfully, and at the appropriate time (but nevertheless promptly).

Special care needs to be taken with any students who will be named. They should be given advance notice—at least a day or two, if possible—of what information will be made public, and when, where, and how it will be presented. Except in highly unusual cases, if the disclosure will be made in a community meeting, they should be invited, but not required, to be at the meeting. Leaders also need to assure them that, at such a meeting, they won't allow attacks, insults, or accusations. (And at the beginning of this meeting, they need to publicly insist that community members uphold this principle.)

At most, community leaders should delay their disclosure of names for a few days. This allows the student(s) who will be named to prepare for the emotional thunderstorm to come. It also enables the student(s) to privately, and in advance, disclose the information to whomever they choose.

When requests for silence or anonymity are honored for more than a very brief period, even out of respect or compassion for victims, this can easily deepen existing wounds. Paradoxically, it can also protect the transgressing teacher—and it can even enable his continued misconduct.

Withholding names can also create a welter of doubt and suspicion, especially if there are conflicting accounts of what happened. *Let me get this straight. You're accusing Guru-ji of seducing four of his students, but you're not going to reveal any of their names, and Guru-ji himself denies that he did any of it.* It's a perfect crazy-making setup. Everyone in the community quickly intuits that one of three things is happening: (1) the spiritual teacher is lying and keeping secrets; (2) community leaders are lying and keeping secrets; (3) *both* are lying and keeping secrets. Much suffering will likely follow, and the spiritual community may be torn to bits.

Speaking up can be difficult and painful. Blowing the whistle on misconduct is also hard. Both can result in blame, scapegoating, lost status, and lost friends. Speaking up is especially hard when a good friend who has been the victim of an exploitive spiritual teacher asks for silence or anonymity. This creates a painful and difficult choice, between supporting a beloved friend and supporting a beloved community. Yet for the community's ultimate health, and for the safety of its current and future members, speaking up may be necessary.

Chapter 25

Double Helix or Tug-of-War?: Balancing Spiritual and Organizational Authority

THIS CHAPTER is not an academic examination of organizational dynamics or a manual on how to design an effective administrative structure for a spiritual community. Instead, it's a look at a few simple organizational principles that can keep spiritual communities healthy—and that will help keep teachers from transgressing.

When a spiritual community is just a handful of like-minded people, it typically functions like an informal club, or a seminar, or a family. Roles may be fluid and temporary. Decisions are usually made by informal consensus, or by individuals on the fly. Any problems that arise can usually be dealt with informally as well. Often these very small organizations are run out of one or two people's heads, hearts, and wallets. All of this works most of the time because there's very little at stake if the organization falls apart.

Once a spiritual community grows beyond a certain size, however, it begins to need a formal organizational structure and the delineation of key people's roles and responsibilities. This is when leaders write bylaws, form a board of directors, create formal membership (and expectations and privileges for members), write job descriptions for volunteers, apply for nonprofit status, and so on.

There's no one-size-fits-all threshold at which this shift in dynamics occurs—but, typically, it happens when a group's committed membership reaches ten to twenty-five people.

At roughly the same time, or soon thereafter, authority needs to be separated in two parallel directions: spiritual and organizational.

The Limits and Liabilities of Authority

We need to grant spiritual teachers the authority they deserve in the areas in which they deserve it—and no more. When it comes to matters of the human heart—and to matters of epistemology, ontology, and living a decent or meaningful life—we should let our teachers wield all their wisdom and grant them a good deal of authority (unless they appear to be misusing that authority). In other matters, however, we would be wise to strictly limit their authority.

If a spiritual teacher wants their community to buy a building, or raise membership dues, or send its executive director to a conference, they shouldn't be able to say, "Make it so," and expect people to jump up and comply. After all, the teacher may know little about building codes, zoning, the average income of members, the cost of attending the conference, and a variety of other relevant matters. Other community leaders and/or organization staff may be well versed in such matters, however. The teacher should thus be required to make a formal request to the relevant person or group, and to accept whatever decision they make.

In a healthy and mature spiritual community, a spiritual teacher holds only one of several top positions. They serve as the community's spiritual director, and accept all of that role's authority and responsibilities. (In communities with multiple teachers, this role may be shared, or there may be one or more head teachers plus one or more junior teachers.) But other folks serve—formally or informally—in the roles of chief operating officer, chief financial officer, and/or executive director. Larger organizations may have other defined roles as well. All of these people, including the spiritual teacher, ultimately report to a governing board, which has the power to hire, retain, and fire the spiritual teacher. The board also creates job descriptions for the teacher, other employees, and volunteers. Members of this governing board are elected by community members.

The spiritual teacher may or may not be a part of that board, but they should have no voting privileges on it; this protects the community in the event that an exploitive teacher attempts to sway the board in a dysfunctional direction. In parallel fashion, the governing board should have no power to dictate to the spiritual teacher what or how to teach, so long as they follow their job description. (The board can, however, make requests and suggestions, which the teacher is not obliged to follow.)

Many dysfunctional spiritual communities have no such separation of powers. The spiritual teacher wields complete, unrestricted authority on all matters, and their word on every subject is law. There may be a governing board and/or an executive director, but everyone ultimately reports, either officially or unofficially, to the teacher. This is a setup for short-sightedness, narcissism, and abuse of power, because it grants the teacher decision-making authority in areas where they may not be especially wise, informed, or even reasonable. Worse, it may *require* the teacher to make decisions on concerns that would be best left to other, better-informed folks.

Authority is not always a blessing; it can just as easily be a curse. When we give spiritual teachers authority that's too wide in its scope, we unnecessarily burden them, set them up for failure, and make our spiritual communities (and ourselves) vulnerable to harm. Over time, we may even encourage our teachers to lose touch with reality.

Some spiritual communities make a different mistake. They establish clearly defined roles and responsibilities and set up a governing board, but they ask the teacher to serve simultaneously as its chief spiritual officer *and* its chief administrator. In theory, a wise and loving teacher with strong administrative skills might be able to handle—and balance—both roles. In practice, however, this rarely works out. Often the two roles are simply too much for one person to handle. The teacher may then fulfill one of the roles admirably, but cut corners on the other. In difficult times and situations, they may give short shrift to *both* roles. At the very least, they may feel overburdened and/or pulled in two directions at once. It's worth noting how this mirrors some of the dual-role issues created when a spiritual teacher and one of their students become lovers.

In those rare cases where someone with broad talents *can* admirably fill both roles at once, they must also resist the temptations of arrogance, narcissism, and power abuse. A fascinating cautionary tale of just such a situation is Michael Downing's *Shoes Outside the Door: Desire, Devotion, and Excess at San Francisco Zen Center.* Downing's book tells the story of Richard Baker, a charismatic Zen teacher who was also a master administrator. Downing relates how, in the 1970s and 1980s, Baker built a small Zen empire; he also pushed people around, spent a lot of Zen Center's money on himself, and had sex with some of his students.

Most good teachers will refuse to take on any authority they can't handle. Over time, however, organizations tend to grow, and as they do, key people's responsibilities and authority can grow as well. What begins as a small and easy-to-handle role can eventually become a stressful, complex, and more-than-full-time job. When a spiritual teacher finds themselves saddled with more authority than they can (or ought to) handle, they should say so publicly, and hand some of that authority back to their community's governing board.

Chapter 26

Why Codes, Policies, and Therapies Aren't Enough

SOME YEARS AGO, when I was a volunteer in charge of ordering books for Dharma Field Zen Center, I was asked to sign a form by the head of Dharma Field's board of directors. The form was a written promise that I would not use my "position of authority" at Dharma Field to sexually exploit anyone. As I handed him the signed form, I said, "It's good that you had me sign this. I had plans to offer people discounts on Buddhist books in exchange for blow jobs—but now, because I've signed this form, I've had to scuttle those plans." He laughed and said, "Yeah, I know, the form is kind of stupid, but it's necessary." Indeed. Stupid, genuinely necessary, and entirely inadequate.

Until the 1980s, few spiritual communities had guidelines, codes, or policies regarding sexual exploitation or the violation of personal boundaries. It simply didn't occur to many community leaders that such things were necessary. Their thinking went like this: *Surely everyone in the community knows which kinds of speech and actions are okay, and which ones aren't. People don't need an instruction manual for being part of a spiritual community. After all, they don't need one for riding a bus or entering a building.*

This reasoning is wrong on all counts. We *do* need instructions for riding buses, which is why signs tell us not to eat, drink, smoke, or play radios, and implore us to let elderly and handicapped people have the seats near the front. Many buildings do have entry instructions posted near the doors: *no smoking; no firearms; no pets; no shirt or shoes, no service;* or, in the case of Dharma Field, *Please remove your shoes.* Even the doors themselves often have instructions: *push; pull.* In order to coexist, we need to give each other instructions all the time. *Right turn on green arrow only. Please turn off your cell phone. Pick up after your pet.*

In the 1980s, in the wake of hundreds of sex scandals involving spiritual teachers and clergy from a wide range of traditions, many spiritual communities realized that they needed to adopt formal rules, policies, codes, and guidelines regarding sexual conduct. Some of these focused on sex between teachers or clergy and their students or congregants; others dealt with teachers' sexual activity in general; still others addressed the larger issues of exploitation, coercion, manipulation, and the abuse of power. Some policies and codes applied specifically to teachers and clergy; some covered all people in positions of authority (including spiritual teachers, board members, administrators, support staff, and volunteers); and some applied to all community members. Some codes were fairly informal, some quite formal and legalistic.

In general, we need these codes, policies, and guidelines because they remind us of things we may have ignored or forgotten—or may simply need to have reinforced. They also provide clear expectations, and clear grounds for a teacher's removal if he transgresses.

It makes sense to have spiritual teachers, clergy, staff, volunteers, etc., read and sign such guidelines. However, we shouldn't imagine that these efforts are sufficient. Policies and codes, after all, are only as strong as people's willingness to follow and enforce them.

There will always be some folks—including some spiritual teachers, and some students—who will transgress (or try to transgress) no matter what we ask, expect, or demand of them. Thus, the application and enforcement of our codes and policies will always be necessary.

To encourage this, community leaders need to regularly remind members of how its policies and codes serve them; how and why they keep the community healthy; and how every community member is responsible for living up to them. These reminders should highlight specific, practical benefits, actions, and examples. They should also acknowledge that living by these codes and policies often requires mindfulness, courage, and discernment. Most important of all, leaders must regularly model the actions they want to encourage in community members.

Of course, no code or policy can replace—or create—a healthy and loving spiritual community. A deeply dysfunctional community will tend to encourage its teacher to lose their way, no matter what its written policies and guidelines say; a sane and compassionate community will encourage its teacher—and its members—to act wisely, even if some people fail to keep its formal policies in mind.

A Few Guidelines on Guidelines

This book isn't the place for a detailed discussion on creating effective codes, policies, and guidelines. Still, it's wise to briefly note a few general principles:

▸ At all times, keep in mind that the purpose of community guidelines (like the purpose of this book) is to encourage greater safety and spiritual intimacy between teachers and students, and among community members.

▸ Good policies and guidelines walk a clear and consistent middle path. Don't assume that spiritual teachers don't need guidance—but also don't assume that they're all potential exploiters, errants, or exceptionalists.

▸ The best policies and guidelines are simple, clear, straightforward, and, of course, written down. Don't overengineer them or try to cover every possible contingency (though some specific details and examples can be helpful). "We all agree to do no harm" is clear, concise, and elegant. So is "We will consistently practice openness and transparency in our governance."

▶ Policies should specifically discuss the conduct the community expects from its spiritual teachers, leaders, and members—and the conduct it prohibits. These should include clear policies about sexual relationships between teachers and students. (For example: *If two people in a teacher-student relationship begin to become romantically involved, a choice must be made between either pursuing that romantic relationship or continuing the teacher-student relationship, but not both.*) Some spiritual communities may wish to set clear policies about sexual relationships between students and nonteaching community leaders as well.

▶ If a community wishes, policies might also speak to teachers' sexual relationships in general (e.g., they will be expected to be monogamous, they must be either married or celibate, etc.).

▶ Just as it's essential to create a plan for dealing with a potential fire, flood, or other emergency, it's essential to have clear guidelines and procedures in place for dealing with a teacher's misconduct *before* something goes wrong. These guidelines and procedures will be extremely difficult to create on the fly if the community is in crisis. If these are in place in advance, community leaders will know what to do and expect during a time of great stress and confusion. Community members will also have some security and protection in the midst of enormous uncertainty.

▶ Every spiritual community would also do well to keep on hand FaithTrust Institute's *Responding to Clergy Misconduct* and/or the Alban Institute's *When a Congregation Is Betrayed*, edited by Beth Ann Gaede. Leaders can consult these useful, important books as needed.

▶ It is also wise to have in place a clear procedure for making formal complaints—in particular about a teacher's behavior, but also about anything else a community member might perceive as unfair, unwise, unethical, or inappropriate. At minimum, this procedure should state how and to whom the complaint should be delivered, and what the governing board is required to do in response to it.

▶ Policies should be easy for anyone to access on the organization's website. Printed copies should also be available to all who ask for them. It's also a good idea to post these on a bulletin board in a common area.

The Limits of Counseling

If a spiritual teacher transgresses, we can't just ship him off to counseling, therapy, spiritual rehab, or some other form of "treatment," and then welcome him back a few months later as a safe, improved version 2.0 of himself.

Certainly counseling with a good therapist can be very helpful for a spiritual teacher who has lost his way, just as it can for almost anyone who has harmed others. But it's not a magic pill or potion. It doesn't make him all better in the same way that surgery can repair a faulty heart valve. Without the teacher's own earnest and ongoing effort, as much compassion and humility as he can muster, and the loving and consistent support of community members, he may once again lose his footing on the same slippery slope as before.

We also need to examine the role of the spiritual community in the teacher's misconduct. Did we students encourage or enable his actions, wittingly or unwittingly? If so, have *we* changed in ways that will keep us from encouraging or enabling his future misconduct? Or do we continue to encourage (or even create) the same temptations and pressures that he succumbed to before? If the answer to this last question is yes, then we have some difficult work of our own to do.

Chapter 27

Building a Healthy
Spiritual Community

THE HEALTH of any spiritual community depends in part on its teacher, whose actions, words, values, and approach to life will reverberate throughout the community's culture. The converse is also true: spiritual teachers need the sane support of their students and communities. When such support is absent or in short supply, teachers are much more likely to lose their way.

In Chapter 24 I offered a brief definition of a healthy spiritual community. Here is a useful addendum to that definition:

Healthy spiritual communities live by two essential principles:

▸ Spiritual teachers are normal human beings. They may be wise, but they are not infallible.
▸ Community members are responsible to one another. They trust and respect each other, and agree to not harm one another.

Not coincidentally, these are also two of the essential principles undergirding any healthy teacher-student relationship.

The ongoing application of these principles typically endows a spiritual community with these attributes:

- ▶ Recognition of each member's humanity—and their individuality.
- ▶ Recognition of each member's full inclusion in the community.
- ▶ Transparency and openness.
- ▶ A willingness of all members (including the teacher) to be respectfully challenged, questioned, and criticized—and to respectfully challenge or question others.
- ▶ A willingness of all members (including the teacher) to be wrong, to admit mistakes, and to learn from those mistakes.
- ▶ A willingness of all members (including the teacher) to change and grow.
- ▶ A clear, simple mission that is reflected in what community members actually do and say.
- ▶ Very clear, very public expectations of the teacher.
- ▶ Clear job descriptions for the teacher, other employees, and long-term volunteers.
- ▶ Clear and explicit terms of governance.
- ▶ Financial stability.

If a spiritual community falls short of this list of ideals, however, its members needn't feel stuck or ashamed. It's entirely possible for less-than-healthy spiritual communities to become healthier over time by making concerted efforts to change.

In fact, there are consultants who specialize in guiding such changes. Information on some of the most experienced ones appears in the Recommended Resources section at the back of this book.

It's of course also quite possible to improve (or maintain) the health of a spiritual community without bringing in an outside consultant. FaithTrust Institute (faithtrustinstitute.org), for example, regularly offers a two-day ecumenical workshop called "Healthy Boundaries for Clergy and Spiritual Teachers" in multiple locations. It also publishes *A Sacred Trust*, an ecumenical curriculum on student-teacher boundaries that includes DVDs, handbooks, participant workbooks, a facilitator's guide, and ancillary brochures for community members. I strongly encourage leaders of all spiritual communities to provide their teachers—and, ideally, themselves as well—with some form of this training.

The health of a spiritual community is built both from the top down and from the bottom up. To help us students be more aware of healthy boundaries, Zen teacher Jan Chozen Bays regularly leads workshops on sexual vs. nonsexual touch, communication, and energy. These workshops, which are specifically designed for members of spiritual communities, focus on those mental and emotional habits that can—wittingly or unwittingly—sexualize a variety of encounters.

Two Exemplary Cases

To see more clearly how a spiritual community can move from dysfunction to health, let's look briefly at two such transformations. Each organization went through a major crisis, slogged through a period of decline or dissolution, and, over time, successfully reinvented itself.

Our first example is San Francisco Zen Center, which I wrote of briefly in Chapter 25. During the early 1980s, the actions of its abbot, Richard Baker, plunged Zen Center into confusion and pandemonium, and almost blew the organization to pieces. But in late 1983, Baker wrote an open letter of apology to the Zen Center community and resigned as abbot. Zen Center then began a long and painful process of organizational rehab. As Michael Downing observes,

> No one trusted the hierarchical structure of the community, and there was no precedent in the annals of Zen Center—or the history of Zen Buddhism—for representative self-government.... the number of committees and meetings seemed to increase exponentially; the Abbot's Council, officers, and practice committees had ongoing business and new duties during the interregnum, and there were new, ad hoc and restructuring committees...as

well as designated "small groups" of community members that met every two weeks to discuss the fate of Zen
Center, not to mention community-wide workshops and
seminars with psychological counselors and management
consultants. For dozens of senior priests, there were also
weekly appointments with psychotherapists...

It took many years, but Zen Center gave itself an almost-complete
makeover. In 1986, its board of directors gave up their lifetime
appointments (which had created an additional set of organizational problems) and were replaced by elected representatives. A
few years later, the position of abbot was changed from an appointment for life to a rotating position; beginning in 1995, the abbot
position became shared by two people, with each person serving a
term of three to five years. Detailed codes of conduct were written
and published (most notably "The Ten Essential Precepts," which
appears on San Francisco Zen Center's website), and an ethics and
reconciliation council was established to deal with complaints.

Today, the organization is not without problems, but it has successfully transformed itself from a spiritual dictatorship into a representative spiritual democracy.

In the 1990s, Kripalu Center for Yoga and Health went through
similar scandals—and a similar transformation. Founded in 1972
by charismatic yoga teacher Amrit Desai and a handful of his students, the original Kripalu was a small yoga retreat center in eastern Pennsylvania. Kripalu soon grew into a full-fledged ashram
that offered classes in yoga, holistic health, and Hindu philosophy.
Under Desai's guidance as guru and spiritual leader, Kripalu continued to grow rapidly, moving in 1983 to a former Jesuit seminary
in Massachusetts.

During the 1980s, Desai became an internationally known
spiritual teacher and speaker; Kripalu also became quite successful,
with nearly a thousand visitors a month. Desai was the unquestioned
top dog at Kripalu, whose nearly three hundred residents viewed
him as holy (or, according to Kripalu's website, omniscient). At this

same time, the ashram became a formal church and religious order. Desai required ashram residents to live very simply—and, if they were single, to practice celibacy—even though Desai himself was married with three children and received a handsome salary.

In 1994, community members learned that Desai had had sex with several women who lived at the ashram; other abuses of his power soon came to light as well. Kripalu's board of trustees called for Desai's resignation, and he stepped down, wrote letters of apology to ashram residents, and left the community.

Over the next two years, the ashram gradually disbanded, and a group of over one hundred former residents filed a class action suit against Kripalu. The suit was eventually settled for over $2.5 million.

However, a small group of residents decided that they wanted to keep Kripalu alive. Led by a professional management team, these residents restructured the organization from the ground up. In 1999, Kripalu ceased being a religious order and became a standard nonprofit organization. It continued to offer instruction in Kripalu Yoga, but also began offering a broad range of classes, programs, and retreats from multiple spiritual traditions. Today, Kripalu has become an internationally known—and democratically run—center for yoga, spirituality, and health.

Chapter 28

Hiring a Spiritual Teacher: Mindful Guidance for Spiritual Communities

THIS CHAPTER is not a mini-manual for hiring spiritual teachers. It simply presents some guidelines to help spiritual communities identify (and cull) those teachers who are likely to sexually transgress.

There's no one way in which people become spiritual teachers. Some go through formal training programs that lead to official certification, just as people do to become licensed social workers, opticians, or cosmetologists. Others are clergy (or former clergy) who take on spiritual teaching roles. Still others receive endorsement to teach from their own teachers after years of spiritual mentoring. And some folks simply declare themselves to the world ("I'm a spiritual teacher, and I'm open for business") in much the same way that writers, artists, and musicians often do.

There's no one way in which spiritual teachers become leaders of spiritual communities, either. In many cases, spiritual teachers create communities of students around themselves. In others, students form spiritual communities around their teachers. Sometimes spiritual teachers inherit their community roles, by right of succession or birth; in other cases, they are appointed to these roles. And sometimes they formally apply for jobs as spiritual teachers, and are interviewed and hired by committees, in the same way that social workers, opticians, and cosmetologists are. In these cases, potential candidates may come from within a spiritual community, from outside it, or both.

Doing an executive search for a spiritual teacher isn't as unusual as it sounds. Quite a few established spiritual communities need to do it, for a variety of reasons. For example, a founding teacher retires, dies, or leaves the community to teach elsewhere, but doesn't appoint a successor. Or a community doubles in size, or adds a location in another city, making the spiritual teacher's job too big for one person—but no one from the community has the teacher's endorsement to teach. Or, as we have seen, a spiritual teacher steps down because of a sexual transgression—or because they make a clear and public choice of a romantic relationship with a student over their role as a teacher.

A quick reminder: despite the great power differential between a spiritual teacher and each of their students, *collectively* we students have ultimate power over our teachers. We have the power to choose them; the power to hire or approve them; the power to dismiss them; the power to support them; and the power to abandon them. In many cases we can abandon them formally, as San Francisco Zen Center and Kripalu did. In all cases, however, we can also do it informally and individually, as many thousands of students have done, by simply walking away or turning our attention elsewhere.

The guidelines that follow apply primarily to spiritual communities that plan to interview and hire new teachers. However, most of the guidelines can also be used to evaluate a potential teacher who has already been recommended or endorsed for the role.

> ▶ Every spiritual community big enough to have a governing body, whether formal or informal, should have a clear written job description for its spiritual teacher(s), written by that governing body. This job description should clarify what the

spiritual community stands for and what it expects from a teacher.

▶ This job description also should clearly specify what sexual activity the community will accept from the teacher, and what it won't. These do's and don'ts need to take a middle path between meaningless generalities ("the teacher will model loving and appropriate sexual behavior at all times") and ludicrous specificity ("the teacher may not engage in bestiality, necrophilia, pederasty, group sex..."). Something like this works well: "The teacher must be either celibate or married and faithful to their partner." So does this: "The teacher may have a partner or be in a monogamous unmarried relationship. The teacher may not engage in open marriage, sex outside of a monogamous relationship, or sex with any of their students."

▶ A teacher's acceptable sexual behavior should be designated *as a condition of their employment.* If a teacher does sexually transgress—or become accused of sexual misconduct—the governing body can thus temporarily take them off the job without first having to address questions of ethics, fairness, extenuating circumstances, etc. This is precisely what an employer would do with a bus driver who comes to work seemingly drunk, or an airline gate agent who arrives at work hallucinating and shouting. Leaders' immediate concern should be with community members' safety.

▶ It is also an excellent idea to include in each spiritual teacher's job description a version of the physicians' oath, e.g., "The teacher vows first to do no harm."

▶ Interviews with potential teachers should frankly and straightforwardly address many of the issues discussed in this book. Each candidate should be asked many questions that begin, "How would you handle...?" These questions should involve students' projections, attempted manipulation, attempted seduction, sexual confessions, emotional outbursts, mental illness, and so on. The teacher should also be asked to role-play some difficult situations, such as a student's attempted seduction or another student's sudden rage or hysteria.

▸ Potential teachers should also be asked, quite directly: "Have you ever been accused of sexual misconduct? If so, tell us what happened. Give us specific events and details." This question may create some initial discomfort, but it needs to be asked, as part of the governing body's due diligence. (If the question *isn't* asked, the teacher is brought on board, and they later sexually transgress, the community may be held liable for *not* asking it.)

▸ Interviewees should also be asked, equally directly: "What is your view on sexual relationships between spiritual teachers and their students?" and "Have you ever had sex with any of your students?" These questions won't weed out all the potential transgressors, of course, but they may help to identify a few, and will likely discourage some others from taking (or continuing to seek) the position. The question will also get the topic out into the open, and help everyone become more comfortable with talking about it.

▸ If a potential teacher has been the subject of any allegation of sexual misconduct, the community's governing body should look into it with diligence, depth, and care. In cases where allegations of misconduct come from multiple people—even if all those allegations were later disproven or withdrawn—this should be considered a huge red flag.

▸ Consider an equally large *yellow* flag to be raised if a potential teacher responds with great emotional force to one or more of the above questions. It makes no difference whether their over-the-top response relates to themselves ("How dare you even raise the issue!"; "Of course not; I'd slit my wrists before I'd do such a thing!") or to other teachers ("They may call themselves spiritual teachers, but they're just rutting animals with no self-control"; "Teachers who have sex with their students belong in the ninth circle of Hell"). Sadly, teachers who have the loudest and angriest reactions to others' sexual misconduct often lose their own way later.

These minimal guidelines are far from sufficient, of course. The issues discussed here form only one small piece of a much larger puzzle: Is the teacher wise, honest, forthright, compassionate, and fully present? Will they inspire—and challenge—the community and its members to do and be their best? Do they routinely walk their talk? When they do talk, do they speak to people's hearts?

Like members of all other professions, spiritual teachers range from wonderful to awful. First-rate teachers are rare. Finding—and, in some cases, even recognizing—such a teacher may take a good deal of time, effort, and diligence. However, as with many aspects of the spiritual life, the seemingly slow and difficult path usually turns out to be the most direct—and attempted shortcuts often lead to suffering and disappointment.

Chapter 29

Building Support Systems
for Spiritual Teachers

WE HUMAN BEINGS need each other. We especially need trustworthy people we can turn to and talk to when times get tough or our emotions threaten to get the best of us. In a serious pinch, one such person will do, but in an ideal world each of us would have a cadre of these folks.

Many students assume that their spiritual teachers don't need such confidants. "She's fully enlightened. Why would she need someone's help? Anyone she talked to would have less insight than her." This belief could not be more off the mark. It's like wondering why a talented surgeon would ever need an operation, or why a great chef would go out for beer and pizza.

As we've seen over and over in this book, spiritual teachers are fundamentally no different from other human beings. Many have more insight and compassion than most people—but they usually have more responsibilities, stresses, temptations, and difficult choices as well. As a result, they need safety valves, sounding boards, confessors, and advisors as much as their students do.

Yet, all too often, spiritual teachers *don't* have anyone they can complain to, confess to, or ask for guidance or support. This isolation can be a recipe for trouble.

For starters, most spiritual teachers need someone they can go to now and then just to blow off steam. Often it's pretty hot steam: "One of my students keeps trying to seduce me. He also keeps trying to annoy my wife, and after three months he's finally starting to succeed." "No matter how many times I explain that our tradition is about service rather than pleasing ourselves, almost nobody seems to get it." "People think I can perform miracles. Meanwhile they ignore the ongoing miracle all around them." "I really wish people would stop trying to make me their surrogate parent."

More importantly, spiritual teachers need peers or colleagues to whom they can go for guidance and advice. We students often imagine that our teachers always know the right choice to make or the right thing to do or say. Sometimes they do. At other times, though, they can get stuck or confused—or may simply not know what to do. Consulting with trusted confidants can help them move beyond their confusion, uncertainty, and narrow straits.

We students generally can't—and shouldn't—serve as our teachers' confidants or counselors. However, lots of other people can. Let's look at who these folks are and how they can help.

Trusted Colleagues

Spiritual teachers define *colleague* or *peer* in multiple ways. For one teacher, it might mean other teachers and clergy from the same tradition or teaching lineage. For another, it might mean a very small handful of specific teachers in their tradition whom they respect and admire. For yet another, it might be a group of insightful teachers from a variety of traditions. However a teacher may define these terms, they can benefit greatly from close relationships with a small number of colleagues they trust. These relationships can be especially valuable in times of crisis or great stress, for the teacher can simply pick up the phone, dial a number, and say, "Hi. It's Sandy. I'm in trouble and I need your help."

Some of these peer relationships evolve naturally. But teachers would be wise to deliberately build more of them. The first step can be as simple as introducing themselves in a phone call or email and asking to have an initial conversation.

It's also enormously helpful for spiritual teachers to meet regularly—at least once a quarter, and ideally once a month—with small groups of their peers (say, five to fifteen people). These groups would roughly mirror the peer support groups of psychologists, social workers, physicians, clergy, and other helping professionals. Most meetings would be devoted to informal discussions of whatever issues or concerns the teachers have at the time. Participants could raise questions, ask for advice or referrals (and, sometimes, for empathy and commiseration), or simply reveal what's on their minds and in their hearts.

Meetings should be strictly confidential, so that teachers can feel free to speak the unspeakable. "Sometimes I just want to chase all of my students away and start over." "I've gotten more and more impatient with students who keep endlessly repeating the same mistake. Last week, while answering a question after a talk, I almost shouted at someone, 'You know what? JUST GROW UP!' Has anyone here had an experience like this?" "This one student keeps making eyes at me—and part of me just wants to jump her bones." At minimum, saying such things to one's empathetic peers releases internal pressure. At best, it also elicits valuable guidance and support.

While many such groups will meet in offices and conference rooms, they can also meet in cyberspace, via videoconferencing or on conference calls.

Unfortunately, as of now, very few peer support groups exist for spiritual teachers. It's time to start forming more of them.

The Teacher's Teacher

Many spiritual teachers continue to have teachers or mentors of their own. This is not a mark of spiritual immaturity, since in matters of the spirit there is no completion, only an ever-deepening awareness. In fact, it's a mark of spiritual immaturity—and perhaps narcissism as well—when a teacher thinks, "I've gone as far as it's possible to go. I don't need anyone's guidance or advice." As Zen teacher Yvonne Rand observes, "Teachers who don't regularly sit in the student seat are likely to run into issues of abuse of power or boundary violations."

A teacher's own teacher or mentor can be an ideal source of advice, guidance, empathy, reality checks, and, sometimes, kicks in the butt. ("Welcome to the job of spiritual teacher! Did you really think that student wasn't going to lie to you and your husband? Wake up and smell the coffee, *sensei*!")

Professional Counselors

Almost any good professional counselor will be very familiar with the problems outlined in this book, partly from personal experience. Whether their training is in psychology, social work, ministry, or some combination, counselors can help spiritual teachers get through trying times without going ballistic or losing their way. They can also help teachers examine any larger personal issues that may bubble up in the process.

Some students may have trouble accepting that their beloved guru, swami, lama, or master needs their head shrunk. ("But she's the living embodiment of wisdom! How can she need a therapist?") These students should be gently reminded that, like them, their teacher is a human being who at times also needs to see a physician, a dentist, and an eye doctor.

Outside Confidants

In a perfect world, each spiritual teacher would also have at least one personal confidant: someone they trust deeply and can be completely candid with—and who is not part of their spiritual community. Typically, this is a good friend or a close relative.

This confidant can offer not only wisdom and support, but an invaluable outsider's perspective. They can thus help bring the spiritual teacher back down to earth; let them know when they've gotten caught up in a dysfunctional group dynamic; and tell them when they're foolish, short sighted, narrow minded, or full of crap. The ideal such confidant is loving, open-minded, and not part of the teacher's spiritual tradition—or, perhaps, any spiritual tradition at all.

The teacher's spouse or partner can of course be such a confidant. However, their partner is usually a community insider—and, thus, may have a personal stake in some of the issues their partner wants to discuss. The teacher's partner may also have some of their own issues with students and/or the community as a whole.

Review Boards

Another important piece of the support puzzle is a professional review board: an organization that sets, upholds, and enforces standards of conduct among spiritual teachers (and, usually, community leaders) within a particular sect, denomination, or tradition. A review board has the power to call a teacher on the carpet for misconduct—and, when appropriate, to reprimand them, sanction them, or remove them from their teaching role. A review board also serves another important function: students can appeal to it if they feel they've been harmed, but their complaints have not been adequately handled within their spiritual communities.

Physicians, social workers, psychologists, and most other helping professionals have such review boards. Spiritual teachers need them, too, to provide some tough consequences for those who transgress—and to support those who don't.

Most of the major Abrahamic religious denominations already have such boards to oversee and enforce standards among their clergy. Spiritual teachers who are active clergy in these denominations normally answer to these boards.

However, many smaller sects and denominations don't yet have these boards—either for clergy, spiritual teachers, or both. Many sects and denominations in the non-Abrahamic traditions

(Buddhism, Hinduism, Sikhism, Jainism, Bön, etc.) don't have them, either, at least here in the West. Consider these words a vigorous call to establish them.

A Live Hotline

One of the most potentially useful—and transgression-preventing—forms of support for spiritual teachers would be a telephone hotline that's answered by a live, anonymous person. In my view, the need for such a hotline is urgent—but, as of now, spiritual teachers don't have one.*

Teachers could call this hotline when they are hurting, upset, confused, under immense pressure, sorely tempted to do something that may cause harm, or needing to talk about the harm they have already caused. This hotline should be confidential, open 24/7, and staffed by volunteers who are themselves first-rate spiritual teachers. A similar service using instant messaging instead of a phone line might also be set up in cyberspace.

This hotline needn't be in a single physical location. It can be a simple network of spiritual teachers with cell phones who volunteer to help for two to three hours per week, plus a part-time traffic manager who oversees the network and does the scheduling. The cost of establishing and maintaining such a hotline would be relatively small, since it could be staffed entirely by volunteers and would use simple, readily available technology.

It wouldn't be difficult for an organization—say, a spiritually-oriented nonprofit or a national church office—to set up such a hotline. Indeed, one ambitious, detail-oriented person could get such a hotline up and running in ninety days. Thereafter, the primary

---

*Currently, Zen teacher Jan Chozen Bays routinely (and informally) fields calls from Buddhist, Hindu, and other Eastern-tradition teachers facing trouble or crises. I applaud her efforts, but obviously one wise and generous volunteer can't do it all. Spiritual teachers need a more formal and organized hotline that will be available 24/7, that can serve teachers from all traditions (as well as teachers from outside the major traditions), and that can be widely publicized among spiritual teachers and their communities.

operational tasks would be recruiting and scheduling volunteers. This might be a half-time job at most.

Ideally, each spiritual tradition, denomination, or teaching lineage will soon have its own hotline. However, an ecumenical hotline can also work passably well, provided it is staffed by spiritual teachers who take an ecumenical approach and are reasonably well trained in world religions.

Once such a hotline has been set up, it can be easily expanded to serve several other groups: (1) students who have become sexually involved with their spiritual teachers; (2) students whose spiritual teachers have attempted to seduce or manipulate them; (3) students who have become uneasy about their teachers, and who sense that a potential seduction may be forthcoming; and (4) students who feel powerfully attracted to their teachers, and who are having trouble maintaining their own sexual boundaries.

Where Support Begins

The ultimate responsibility for providing support to any spiritual teacher rests with the teacher themselves. Each must build their own support network, piece by piece, and weave them together into a coherent whole. No one else can—or should try to—do this for them.

Creating such a support network is an expression of a teacher's love and caring for themselves. These are as important as their love and caring for their students.

Chapter 30

Training, Encouraging, and Culling Potential Teachers

THE TRAINING of spiritual teachers differs widely from tradition to tradition, group to group, and even teacher to teacher. In many cases it is quite formal and programmatic, with clear steps, benchmarks, and decision points. In others it is a fluid, informal part of a one-to-one relationship between a spiritual teacher and their protégé.

Almost nobody trains to become a spiritual teacher in the same way that people train to become engineers or welders or accountants. People don't become spiritual teachers to earn big bucks, or because they want reliable jobs and incomes,* or because it's indoor work that doesn't require Excel or QuickBooks skills. Nor do college students visit career counselors and ask, "How can I break into the dynamic profession of spiritual teaching?"

Instead, spiritual teachers typically feel called to the role, often in spite of their own desires and objections. They must also possess a special talent for listening, observing, and empathizing. And they must have a great deal of insight, patience, and love for their fellow human beings.

---

* In practice, few spiritual teachers make lots of money or enjoy a great deal of job security. Those few people who do hope to acquire wealth or security by becoming spiritual teachers thus tend to be charlatans, predators, or foolish narcissists.

196 Sex and the Spiritual Teacher

However, not everyone with these qualities is suited to be a spiritual teacher. As we saw in earlier chapters, some people have personal limitations that make them likely to transgress or melt down during times of great difficulty, stress, and/or temptation. These folks need to be spotted as early in their training as possible, and their limitations need to be fully addressed. In many cases, this means encouraging (or requiring) people to get some focused counseling or training from a professional (e.g., a psychotherapist, a presentation skills trainer, etc.). In other cases, it means clearly and deliberately steering people away from any spiritual teaching role.

The Power of Mentoring

A small percentage of legitimate spiritual teachers—and a high percentage of less-than-legitimate ones—receive no formal training or endorsement from others; they simply declare themselves to be teachers. Eckhart Tolle, Byron Katie, Lee Lozowick, and quite a few others began their careers as spiritual teachers in this way. In such cases, of course, not much can be done to get a vulnerable teacher to shore up their weaknesses—or to convince them that they shouldn't be spiritual teachers at all.

However, if a potential teacher is engaged in formal study or training—or has a close relationship with a teacher of their own—then many opportunities exist to help them make wise decisions and choices.

Mentoring is the key. We've all heard stories of people who fell through cracks in systems and ended up harming others. In training spiritual teachers, all such cracks can and should be tightly sealed—and mentoring is the primary process for spotting and sealing them.

Whether a potential teacher is a spiritual teacher's sole protégé or one of hundreds of people in a large seminary or training program, each potential teacher should have a mentor who oversees their training. This can of course be their own spiritual teacher, but it does not have to be.

In the paragraphs that follow, I'll discuss what this mentoring might look like, based on some of the best practices in psychology, social work, education, spiritual leadership, and other helping professions. I offer these ideas as suggestions, not prescriptions—and as places to start rather than as a detailed program.

Throughout mentees' training, I suggest that they and their mentors meet one-on-one at least every other month for sixty to ninety minutes. Meetings should include lots of role playing, plenty of thought experiments ("What will you do when..."), and ample time for the mentee to ask questions and request guidance.

Mentors should also regularly remind mentees, "This isn't hypothetical stuff. It happens all the time, and it's always difficult." They should also tell relevant stories: "Let me tell you about two of the times this happened to me, and how in one case I was totally blindsided, and acted badly as a result." "This happened to my colleague Sheila just last month. Here's how she handled it..."

Every few months, mentors and mentees should also have discussions that deeply explore, and re-explore, the question, "Why do you see yourself becoming a spiritual teacher?" Based on the mentee's answers and personality, the mentor can then provide hand-tailored guidance for spotting and avoiding potential problems.

Throughout the process, an essential part of the mentor's job is to observe the mentee, note their potential vulnerability to the temptations described in this book, and discuss the relevant issues with them, honestly and directly. The mentor should also encourage their mentee to express their own concerns about their potential vulnerabilities or limitations.

If a mentor feels their mentee may be unable to handle the stresses and temptations of being a spiritual teacher, they should urge the mentee to get professional help (psychological counseling, etc.), to abandon their plans to become a spiritual teacher, or both. As appropriate, the mentor can also suggest other possible professional endeavors, such as spiritual speaking, writing, or scholarship—or work in unrelated fields.

If the mentee refuses or ignores their mentor's advice, the mentor shouldn't shrug, say to themselves, "Well, I did my due diligence," and let the issue drop. Ideally, they should be required to take a further step in the same direction. In the case of formal training programs, this might mean petitioning for the mentee's dismissal, or requiring that the mentee go before an internal review board. In the case of less formal, one-to-one training between a teacher and a protégé, the teacher may need to say, "Until you address this weakness, I'm putting the brakes on your training." Or, perhaps, "We can continue working together as teacher and student, but let me be clear: I'm no longer training you to be a teacher yourself. I don't feel you should become one, and I don't plan to endorse you as one." In certain cases, the teacher may even need to end their teacher-student relationship. Hats off to every teacher who shoulders these difficulty responsibilities.

Like all of us, though, mentors sometimes make mistakes. Once in a while, someone who is discouraged from becoming a spiritual teacher will prove their mentor wrong; they'll become a wise and balanced teacher who serves their students with great compassion and insight. Hats off to these teachers, too, for knowing when to doubt well-meaning but unhelpful guidance.

Beyond Mentoring

Important as mentoring is in preparing and culling spiritual teachers, it should be augmented with relevant classroom training wherever possible.

All formal training programs for potential spiritual teachers should include a full-length course on the temptations and dilemmas that spiritual teachers often face—not just sexual ones, but all the ones involving power, status, student expectations, projection, etc. This course should also include training in boundaries and conflict resolution. (Some seminaries and divinity schools already offer such a course or workshop.) In less formal, one-to-one forms of training, this class might be replaced with a series of regular meetings on the subject, perhaps over coffee or breakfast.

The teacher of this class should be a spiritual teacher who is forthright, honest, accessible, and willing to discuss their own difficulties, failings, and limitations.

It's important that this class treat the *desire* to have sex with students as normal and natural, not a sin or a form of psychological dysfunction. The more that potential teachers see how actions are separate from desires and impulses, the less power those desires and impulses will have for them.

Ideally, guest speakers in this class would include spiritual teachers who talk honestly about their own temptations, difficulties, limitations, failures, or near-failures; at least one student who was exploited, sexually or otherwise, by their spiritual teacher; and at least one student who became sexually involved with their spiritual teacher by mutual consent.

The instructor of this class should observe students carefully. When they spot a likely exploiter, errant, or exceptionalist—or anyone with a notable limitation or vulnerability—they should take that person aside and encourage them to seek professional help, to abandon their plan to teach, or both.

Current spiritual teachers might also be invited to attend this class as members. For these teachers, the class may provide important reminders and guidance, as well as practical strategies for managing their roles and emotions. The presence of current teachers will also help other class members realize that the dynamics of teacher-student relationships are never fully mastered, and can only be handled one relationship, and one encounter, at a time.

In Chapter 29, I presented a variety of things that current spiritual teachers can do to get support, stay sane, and keep from losing their way. Most of these same practices and systems can be equally valuable for future teachers. Indeed, I strongly urge these folks to put personal support systems in place while they are still being trained, so that they have somewhere reliable to turn when they first face big difficulties, tough decisions, or great personal stress.

With this in mind, I also suggest that all formal training programs for spiritual teachers include an ongoing mentoring component for its recent graduates. After someone completes their training, they should be required to continue meeting (in person or by phone) with their mentor at least once every other month, and perhaps more often, for the next year or two. The mentor should also make themselves reasonably available for emergency consultation as needed.

Everything I propose in this chapter will help weed out potential exploiters, errants, and exceptionalists at a relatively early stage. It will also help future teachers with considerable talent but notable weaknesses to notice, understand, and address those weaknesses. But these efforts aren't only meant to have a prophylactic function; they will also help every participant to better handle the stresses and challenges of the spiritual teacher's role.

Chapter 31

When a Spiritual Teacher Transgresses: Responses of a Healthy Community

THIS CHAPTER is a brief look at how community leaders and members can respond with empathy, insight, and compassion when they learn that their spiritual teacher has sexually transgressed—or been accused of transgressing. It does *not* offer a detailed process to follow, for such a process would easily fill a good-sized book. (In fact, FaithTrust Institute has published such a book, *Responding to Clergy Misconduct*. The Alban Institute has published a similar volume, *When a Congregation Is Betrayed: Responding to Clergy Misconduct*, edited by Beth Ann Gaede.)

Even the most thorough book isn't sufficient, however. Unless the teacher's transgression has been minor, the community will also need the help of an experienced and compassionate consultant to guide it through the healing process. (If a spiritual teacher's misconduct is a one-time, short-term misstep and he has not broken a vow of celibacy or fidelity, then an outside consultant may not be necessary—particularly if the misstep is quickly disclosed and appears to do little or no harm to the community. Otherwise, though, a spiritual community that tries to work through the issues without a consultant's help can easily lose its way.)

This consultant needs to come from outside the community—and from outside the authority structure of the spiritual tradition. For example, if a spiritual teacher in an Orthodox Jewish community has transgressed, it's not wise to bring in a consultant from the Union of Orthodox Jewish Congregations. As a part of the Orthodox Union, the consultant may have an interest in creating a particular outcome; they may also have some real, implied, or assumed authority over community members. This interest and authority may get in the way of full disclosure, honest discussion, and healing. However, the community can certainly bring in a Jewish consultant who is outside of the Orthodox power structure.

At first, community leaders are often tempted to try to resolve the matter internally. They'll likely have plenty of reasonable-sounding justifications for doing so: *We're adults—and we're basically healthy. We've got some really good people in key positions, and they're all willing to step up and do their part. We can see our way through this. In fact, working through the issues will help us come together as a community, and make us stronger and more unified. Anyway, it doesn't make much sense to bring in someone who's unfamiliar with our tradition and teaching lineage. Besides, it's nobody's business but our own.*

Reasonable as these ideas may sound, in practice they typically prove inadequate, because they attempt to resolve serious issues by applying the same community norms, structures, and culture that created them. When spiritual communities use this seemingly self-reliant (but, in fact, incestuous) approach, their problems tend to grow. As Candace Benyei notes in *Understanding Clergy Misconduct in Religious Systems*, "[T]he power of family rules within the system, and the subtle coercive forces used to support them, cannot be overemphasized.... Incestuous systems do not heal themselves of their own accord."

A good outside consultant will be able to clearly see things that leaders and members of the community may have become blind to. In addition, the consultant isn't beholden to the community, its spiritual tradition, or the larger system that includes them. The consultant thus has no power to discipline or coerce anyone—nor can anyone in the community coerce them.

But the most important attribute a good consultant can have is their experience. *They have seen similar situations before—perhaps many times.* What may seem so confusing and unclear to community members may be both clear and familiar to the consultant. They will thus often know what steps to take and how to guide the community through them.

In short, a good consultant can offer clarity, insight, understanding, guidance, and, when necessary, temporary and provisional leadership. As Benyei observes, "A consultant does not wave a magic wand but collects data and then supports and guides the [community], enabling the membership to access, strengthen, and use its resources in the healing process."

In general, it's a good idea to look for such a consultant as soon as it becomes clear that harm has been done and the community will need healing. Usually this is very soon after a spiritual teacher first discloses his misconduct; or after someone makes a credible accusation of the teacher; or after an earlier, more doubtful accusation begins to appear credible. The sooner a good consultant can be found—and the sooner the situation is discussed with them—the more likely the community is to hold together through the storms to come.

I list some capable and experienced consultants in the Recommended Resources section at the end of this book. However, this list isn't meant to be exhaustive. Here are some guidelines for finding and choosing a good consultant:

- ▶ Good consultants can be psychologists, social workers, or clergy; many are both clergy *and* mental health professionals.
- ▶ The consultant must have a spiritual orientation, though it needn't be formal or tied to a single tradition. Many good consultants are ecumenical; others are devout members of their own faiths. An ideal consultant belongs to your

community's spiritual tradition, but is not part of its power structure. If you have to choose between an ecumenical outsider and an insider with ties to the spiritual hierarchy, go with the outsider.

▸ Avoid any consultant who is not deeply respectful of your spiritual community and tradition. This includes atheists, agnostics, and some devout members of other traditions. These folks may have significant blind spots—and they may bring their personal agendas to your community's healing process.

▸ Experience matters a great deal. Find someone who has done work in other spiritual communities whose teachers or leaders have sexually transgressed.

How the Healing Process Works

In general, a healthy spiritual community dealing with a teacher's sexual misconduct goes through these phases: shock, dismay, and disillusionment; research and discovery; public disclosure and commentary; healing; reorganization and renewal; and final review. These are generally sequential, but they do partly overlap. There may also be times when the community, or some of its members, need to briefly revisit an earlier phase.

Jan Chozen Bays offers this adjacent view of what a spiritual community's healing process, as guided by a qualified consultant, needs to involve

> a process of testimony and discovery (formerly called investigation), sabbatical for the teacher, at least while discovery is underway, a statement of findings by the consulting group—to be made public...and recommendations by the team for justice-making, restitution and healing work. It also includes working on prevention steps for the future for the affected group: drawing up or revising policies and procedures, ethics statements, plus

group education about boundaries and ethics in spiritual relationships.

Throughout this process, everyone's most important guiding principles need to be these:

- ▸ *Do no harm.*
- ▸ *Keep people safe.*
- ▸ *Keep no secrets.*
- ▸ *Tell the truth.*

Together, these principles can serve as an excellent compass for everyone involved. In those rare cases where two of these principles conflict, community leaders need to compassionately consider what will provide the greatest good; the most safety, health, and healing; and the fewest problems in the long run.

A key secondary principle is: *let everyone speak up and be heard.* In times of confusion and upheaval, people need to express themselves. They also need to know that their leaders are paying attention and can be trusted. Anyone who feels silenced or ignored will also feel victimized.

As Marie Fortune notes, the healing of a wounded spiritual community requires these elements:

- ▸ *Truth-telling:* giving voice to the reality of the misconduct.
- ▸ *Acknowledging the violation:* hearing the truth, naming the transgression, and condemning it as wrong.
- ▸ *Compassion:* listening to and suffering with any victims.
- ▸ *Protecting the vulnerable:* taking steps to prevent further transgressions.
- ▸ *Accountability:* confronting the transgressor and imposing negative consequences. This makes repentance possible.
- ▸ *Restitution:* making symbolic restitution of what was lost; providing a tangible means to acknowledge the harm that was done and to bring about healing.

▶ *Vindication:* setting any victims free from the suffering caused by the misconduct.

These elements add up to what Fortune calls *justice-making.*

This process of discovery, commentary, and healing should *never* resemble a trial or an interrogation, and it should not be primarily about the teacher's guilt or innocence; in fact, it should not be primarily about the teacher at all. The focus of the process should always be on the safety, health, and well-being of the community and its members.

Guidelines for Community Healing

Each community's healing process is unique. What follows are general suggestions, not prescriptions; each community, leader, and member will need to adapt them on a case-by-case basis.

When community leaders first learn that their teacher has sexually transgressed—or once they have a credible report of such a transgression—they need to quickly meet and agree on how they will proceed, what their next steps will be, and who will be in charge of what.

One of the governing body's first steps should be to temporarily remove the teacher from his teaching role. This should be done without regard for what he is accused of, or how much proof leaders have. (This mirrors what is done for police officers and schoolteachers who are accused of misconduct.)

This removal must not be merely symbolic; the teacher should be temporarily stripped of all official *and* unofficial authority. This authority should be temporarily assumed by the community's governing body. However, if the teacher receives a salary, he should receive full pay during his temporary removal, so that he is not harmed if the accusation turns out to be false.

Once the teacher has been relieved of his position, community leaders need to quickly and clearly communicate to all members what has happened (i.e., what the teacher has done, or been accused of doing); what the response of the community's governing body has been (i.e., it has temporarily removed the teacher from his position); what will happen next over both the short and long terms; and what the goals of this process are (i.e., safety, healing, reconciliation or resolution, etc.). In the same message, leaders should ask everyone who has information about the teacher's misconduct (or alleged misconduct) to provide it—anonymously, if necessary.

At the same time, however, the governing body needs to make it very clear that the teacher's removal is temporary; that it is not punishment; and, unless the teacher has already admitted misconduct, that it doesn't mean he is guilty of anything. It's simply a way to provide safety for everyone throughout the process of discovery, discussion, and healing.

This message needs to be delivered in multiple ways—through emails, letters, and web pages—to all community members. Clear, widespread communication is essential, so that all community members feel included—and so that the proliferation of rumors is kept to a minimum.

Throughout this entire process, the accused teacher should normally be asked and expected to remain part of the community. This means he should continue to be welcome at services, group meditation, and other community events. In these contexts, he should be given no more (or less) authority, voice, or access to the governing body than any other community member.

However, if at any point the teacher presents a possible danger to anyone—e.g., if he threatens someone, or continues to try to seduce his students, or publicly accuses community leaders of being mentally ill—he may need to be removed from the community, at least for a time.

This is usually the point at which leaders find an outside consultant to help the community through the healing process. At more or less the same time, the governing body should also put together a plan that keeps the organization running relatively smoothly throughout the upcoming discovery, commentary, and healing. This is essential for two reasons: first, the continued presence of a stable organization provides emotional security and balance for community members during this time of upheaval; second, it enables the organization to better weather the emotional storms to come.

In addition, the governing board needs to quickly learn the answers to the following questions, and then to promptly and clearly communicate those answers to all community members:

- ► What is the teacher accused of, and by whom?
- ► Which accusations are true? Which are not? Which are currently debatable or uncertain?
- ► Does the teacher substantially agree with the accusations? If so, does he admit to misconduct?
- ► Has the teacher engaged in any misconduct beyond the initial accusations?
- ► Is the teacher currently in a sexual relationship with any student(s)?
- ► What harm, if any, appears to have been done, and to whom?
- ► Has there been secrecy? If so, how long has it lasted?
- ► Has the teacher violated a vow of celibacy or fidelity?
- ► Has the teacher lied to or misled the community?
- ► Has the teacher been hypocritical—i.e., preached one thing and done another?
- ► If the teacher admits to misconduct, what amends does he propose to make?

At roughly the same time—early in the discovery process—leaders should also organize some public forums. At these, all community members who wish to speak openly should be given the chance to. Each speaker should be encouraged to say whatever they feel moved to say—and promised that they will not be questioned, challenged, heckled, or interrupted. Everyone is asked and expected to simply listen. Members of the governing body should lead these forums, and should respectfully but very firmly enforce the "no questioning, challenging, or interrupting" rule. (This practice has been used, with great success, in Twelve Step groups and healing circles.) In some groups, it may be wise to limit each person's talking time to a few minutes.

During these early phases of the healing process, many community members will feel a strong pull toward hard and fast positions: "They love each other. They're both consenting adults. Stop making a problem out of it." "Throw the scum in jail." "People are out to get Baba because he's so holy and wise. Now they've trumped up this sex scandal." "The asshole destroyed his family. I hope the alimony bankrupts him." "I'm sure Guru-ji had a good reason for what he did. His heart's pure and he's totally beyond sex. He couldn't possibly have a run-of-the-mill fling, especially with a student." "He's sullied the Dharma. I don't want the bastard setting foot in Compassionate Heart Meditation Center ever again." One of the wisest and most stabilizing things community leaders can do during this time is encourage members not to settle into any position, but to stay open, to listen, and to temporarily withhold judgment.

If the spiritual community chooses to hire a lawyer, the lawyer may initially advise leaders to close ranks, withhold information, or further victimize the teacher's accuser(s) by challenging their claims and/or their motives. The lawyer may even urge community leaders to try to eject the accuser(s) from the community. Any of these actions will of course make matters much worse. Yet the lawyer is simply doing their job, as they see it: protecting their client from liability. To prevent such a pernicious turn of events, community leaders need to tell their lawyer from the beginning, "Our goal is not to minimize the organization's liability. It's to heal the community's wounds, keep (or make) it healthy, resolve whatever legal issues arise, and keep people safe. We will not harm or disrespect any human being in order to protect this organization. The interests of community members come before the interests of this nonprofit entity." Because attorneys are rarely asked to think this way, leaders may need to remind their lawyer of this again and again. At times they may need to remind themselves of it as well.

From this point forward, many different scenarios are possible, though the waters the community must sail will almost certainly be turbulent and uncharted. However, a good consultant will have helped other spiritual communities navigate similar rapids, and thus will provide sane and solid guidance.

Each organization needs to chart its own course of healing. However, two approaches are particularly well suited to helping spiritual communities heal in the wake of their teachers' misconduct:

Restorative justice. This is a theory of justice that does not emphasize establishing guilt and meting out punishment, but instead focuses on repairing the harm that someone has caused. It's a cooperative process that typically brings together a transgressor (or multiple transgressors) with victims and community members who wish to be included. In this encounter, people discuss the misconduct and its aftermath, and the transgressor is expected to make amends to repair the harm they have caused. Determining these amends is an integral part of the process. Restorative justice also generally includes restoring victims *and* transgressors to their communities as full, contributing members. Any restorative justice effort needs to be led by an experienced and properly trained facilitator or consultant.

Circles (sometimes called *talking circles* or *healing circles* or *peacemaking circles* or *councils*). This process originated in Native American cultures, but it is now used widely in other contexts and locations. Its theory of justice is virtually the same as that of restorative justice, but its process is more structured and less flexible. A typical circle group includes a transgressor, members of the transgressor's family, the victim(s), members of the victim's family, and community representatives. Everyone sits in a literal circle; each person, one by one, gets to speak about the transgression and its effects. A "talking piece" is passed around; whoever holds it gets to speak, and everyone else must listen respectfully, without interrupting. A keeper (i.e., a facilitator) directs the movement of the talking piece. Once everyone has initially spoken, the group develops a strategy for addressing the transgression. Often the healing process involves multiple circles: one for initial discussion; a second for determining the fate of the transgressor and the amends they will be expected to make; a third to support the healing of any victim(s); and a fourth to support the healing of the transgressor.

Throughout the spiritual community's healing process, the governing body should send out regular updates on what is happening. These should be provided by email and snail mail, and on the organization's website. Printed updates should also be posted on a prominent bulletin board. In such cases it's better to err on the side of overcommunication than to leave anyone wondering.

Community healing takes time. The greater the teacher's misconduct, the longer healing tends to take. One to several years is typical. The process simply can't be rushed, and there are no short cuts. Indeed, attempts to speed up the process are virtually guaranteed to slow it down or grind it to a halt. Some people will complain: "Can't we get past this and move on?" "Enough already! Let's stop dwelling in the past and move forward." "Why are we still swimming around in our old crap?" Community leaders need to let these folks air their complaints, but not be swayed by them. Grief and recovery take time—and they don't respond to reason, optimism, or frustration. Indeed, people who are in a hurry to move on may in fact be unwilling to face their own grief, and trying to leap over it.

Once the healing process is largely complete, the entire community should reconvene to look back at the process and discuss what they did wisely, what mistakes they made, what they might do differently if something similar happens in the future, and what more they can do to prevent future misconduct by a spiritual teacher. Members of the community's governing body should also have their own parallel discussions, which may engender changes in the organization's policies, practices, and/or structure.

Some communities may wish to follow (or combine) the final public review described above with a final open forum, in which anyone who wishes to speak may do so for a few minutes without being questioned, challenged, or interrupted.

When Spiritual Communities Begin to Shatter

In cases where a teacher's transgressions have been large or numerous, the very existence of their spiritual community may be at stake. Some people leave; others take sides; a schism may occur. Leaders and members worry about the community's imminent dissolution, and see this as the worst possible outcome.

Yet this dissolution may be a good thing. The greatest healing sometimes occurs when an organizational structure is forced to collapse so that something saner and healthier can emerge in its place. This is precisely what happened with Kripalu and San Francisco Zen Center.

Furthermore, given the purposes of a spiritual community, it may sometimes be better to sacrifice the organization—which is, after all, nothing more than an elaborate compact among its members—for the safety and well-being of its members. A new organization can always be created, but damage to individual members can never be undone.

Should a Transgressing Teacher Be Reinstated?

There's no formula for determining when a spiritual teacher should be offered his position back; when he should be permanently removed from any teaching role, but permitted (or encouraged) to remain in the community; and when he should be sent packing. Much depends on the form of his transgression, on how the community healing process proceeds, and on what the teacher says and does throughout that process. Nevertheless, a few useful generalities can be noted here.

If community leaders discover that all accusations against the teacher are false, they should promptly reinstate him to his teaching role. Equally promptly, they should send emails and snail mail letters to all community members, explaining what the accusations were, how they were investigated, and how and why they proved baseless. A similar notice should be posted on the organization's website and, in printed form, in a prominent location in a community building. Calling a meeting of the community to present this same information is usually wise as well.

Just because the accusations proved false, however, doesn't mean that the teacher, the community, and its leaders should go back to business as usual. Even unfounded accusations have causes. What can the teacher, the community, and its leaders do to avoid such accusations in the future? What can they learn from what happened, and what can (or should) they do differently going forward?

If the teacher turns out to have been an exploiter, then offering him his teaching role back is clearly unwise. He may be an otherwise insightful and talented teacher, but his very presence in a teaching role conflicts with one of the most essential hallmarks of a healthy spiritual community: safety.

The principle of safety should also be used to determine whether he should be permitted to remain in the community as an ordinary member. For example, a libertine ex-teacher who is unpartnered might pose no problem in some spiritual communities, where he'll just be an ordinary member who likes to sleep around. In other spiritual communities, though—celibate ones, for instance—he'll need to be shown to the door. Charlatans and predators normally need to be booted out; other exploiters can be evaluated on a case-by-case basis.

It's also generally unwise to give long-term errants and exceptionalists, and serial errants and exceptionalists, their teaching jobs back. Their actions strongly suggest that, if reinstated, they will lose their way again, no matter what they promise or vow, and no matter what their job description says. However, in most cases there will be no reason why they cannot remain in the community. The rare exceptions will be obvious.

What of the one-time, short-term errants and exceptionalists— the teachers who made a single sexual misstep, but quickly caught themselves (or were caught by someone else)? It's entirely the community's decision. Certainly no such teacher is automatically *entitled* to resume his teaching role, no matter how penitent he is and no matter what amends he makes. On the other hand, with very few exceptions, he ought to be entitled to remain part of the community as an ordinary member. If he has stepped down but maintains (or wins back) the community's trust over time—after, perhaps, one to three years—and the community wishes to reinstate him, there's arguably no reason why it shouldn't. And, as we have seen, there can be situations in which he (perhaps) needn't step down at all.

In making a decision on reinstating (or keeping) a teacher, spiritual communities would be wise to ask themselves the same two basic questions that inform everything in this book:

1. Is this in students' best interests?
2. Will this help create greater safety and spiritual intimacy between the teacher and students, and among community members?

They would also be wise to seek a clear consensus (though it needn't be a unanimous one) on what the teacher's status will be. Such a consensus strengthens the community, stabilizes it, and reduces the chances of a teacher's transgression in the future.

Chapter 32

An Open Letter
to Spiritual Teachers

TO MANY OF US STUDENTS, your role as a spiritual teacher looks glamorous and exciting—not unlike being a movie star. Some of us, though, realize that your role can sometimes be difficult, painful, frustrating, confusing, tedious, thankless, and lonely.

But whether we're accurate or deluded about your life, all of us want and expect the best from you.

We also want you to encourage the best from us—though you won't always get it. Sometimes we'll project all kinds of things onto you—our hopes, dreams, fears, expectations, and fantasies. It's your job to not buy into any of our projections—and not to do any projecting of your own.

Your role requires you to always act in our best interests. Sometimes this means disappointing or upsetting some of us. Sometimes it means doing the opposite of what we may want, or expect, or ask for. Sometimes it means holding your emotions and actions in check. In each case, we need you to take a deep breath and do what's right.

Over and over, breath by breath, we need you to return to your commitment to serve. If what you're about to do isn't in a student's best interest, don't do it. If you're already doing it, remember your commitment, stop what you're doing, and help keep everyone safe.

To help us not lose our own way, we need you to admit your limitations—publicly, straightforwardly, and often. You will help us the most if you frame each admission not as a confession, but as guidance for what we can and can't (or shouldn't) expect of you. Each admission will also serve as a model for us to follow.

When you don't know something and say "I don't know," this increases, rather than reduces, our trust in you and in your ability to have a positive effect on our lives.

You are an alpha figure—and perhaps the only alpha figure—in our spiritual community. We trust you and depend on you to be honest with us, to guide us, to provide safety (but not comfort), and to consistently put our interests before your own.

Yes, some of us want to have sex with you. A few of us may try to seduce you; others may offer themselves to you. Still others may flirt with you or try to envelop you in sexual energy. Some of us are very aware of our sexual power, and very skillful at using it. Some of us will be enormously aroused by your very ability to rebuff our attempted seductions. Some of us will be turned on by your clothes, your mannerisms, your resemblance to our parents, and other things that have nothing to do with you.

If you are single, some of us will find your availability a huge turn-on, even though we know you're not available to us. If you are celibate or have a partner, some of us will be turned on by your status as forbidden fruit.

A few of us may try to seduce you as a test. In these cases, we see you as a surrogate parent: we trust you deeply, but need to make sure that our trust is deserved. We may try hard to get you to violate that trust, yet what we actually want is for you to keep the sexual boundary in place.

A few of us seek high drama, and will go for the thrill of becoming (or declaring ourselves to be) your victims, no matter what you do or don't do.

When all of this starts to drive you half crazy, we still expect you to love and support us.

You can't stop some of us from doing these things—but you can help us (and yourself) stay safe. You can set clear boundaries, and you can anticipate and avoid potentially dodgy encounters. You may even need to avoid socializing with us outside of large community gatherings such as picnics, fundraising events, and potluck suppers.

As you get older and better known, these temptations and difficulties will probably grow. As a result, over time you will need to make your boundaries continually stronger and clearer.

You cannot do all this alone. No one can. While some of us don't understand this, many of us do. We realize that you can best support us when you ask for the support of our tradition, the wisdom that underlies it, and the people you trust. We also understand that when you turn to your partner, to friends and relatives, to colleagues, to helping professionals, and to your own teacher for this support, you are not turning away from us.

If you have a partner, we need you to love and appreciate them, even though this may make some of us jealous—and even though some of us will project things onto them, just as we do with you.

We want and need you to be in top form. This means we need you to take good care of yourself. Regularly do things that support and feed you—spiritually, physically, and emotionally. Good self-care is far more noble than working yourself sick. It also provides a wholesome and inspiring example for us.

We are always eager to take all you can give, plus much more. So don't expect us to notice when you've reached your limit. You're the one and only person who can keep yourself from becoming depleted. When you pull back, set a boundary, or take a break, we may not like it, but it ultimately helps all of us. So, no matter what we say or ask for, we want you to say "no" to us when your health and sanity require you to.

If you lose your way sexually, don't try to keep the truth from us. You will do the least damage if you go public about it immediately. The sooner you do this, the less pain and harm there will be for everyone, and the easier and more quickly you will find your way back to a centered life. And if you're currently in a secret sexual relationship, don't make us wonder and gossip and worry. Tell us what's going on and face the consequences. This helps everyone—especially us, your students and members of your spiritual community.

If, at some point, your role or situation or obligations genuinely become too much to handle, the best thing you can do for us is to say, "I can't do this any longer," and step down. There is nothing shameful—and much that is noble—in this. You will of course disappoint us. But you will disappoint us far more if you pretend to be someone you aren't—or if you try to do the impossible and fail.

We need you to love us. Not sexually, and not in some idealized, storybook way, but as someone whom we can trust to act in our best interests, over and over. Without this love, you cannot serve wisely.

We also need you to love yourself, for the same reason.

Some Further Questions

A FEW YEARS AGO, at the Shedd Aquarium in Chicago, I spent several minutes staring at a mysterious creature in a tank. I couldn't tell whether it was a fish, an eel, some type of amphibian, or something else entirely. The closer I looked, the more unknown it became.

When a man wearing a Shedd identity card walked past, I stopped him and pointed to the tank. "Can you tell me about that animal? Is it an amphibian? A fish? A reptile? It looks like God took genes from a dozen different creatures and jumbled them together."

The man smiled. "It's a good question," he said, "and the answer is, it doesn't fit anywhere." His smile grew broader. "I'm a grad student in biology at the University of Chicago, and I can tell you this: no matter how detailed we get at categorizing living things, and no matter how carefully we draw a line, we always find a living creature sitting directly on that line, looking up at us and grinning." And then he added, *"Isn't that great?"*

In this book I've made a slew of distinctions, created categories galore, and, I hope, begun to untangle the near-Gordian knot of sexual transgression by spiritual teachers. But please don't think I've provided a detailed formula, recipe, or equation for handling every real-life situation. I haven't. I can't. No one can.

In preventing spiritual teachers' misconduct, and in dealing with it when it occurs, our tools of drawing lines and creating categories will often be inadequate. We will be faced with real human beings, complex situations, and difficult decisions, the outcomes of which will always be uncertain. Often a person or circumstance sits directly on the lines we have so carefully drawn. In these cases, our only wise option is to accept the uncertainty of the situation and act as mindfully and compassionately as we can, step by step and breath by breath.

This book has examined and addressed some vital questions. Yet many other, adjacent questions remain. None of these have one-size-fits-all answers; all must be dealt with on a case-by-case basis, in the here and now. Some examples:

- ▶ If a spiritual teacher has sexually transgressed, but later owns up to his misconduct and makes amends to the people he has harmed, should he be permitted to take up a teaching role in a different spiritual community? If so, how much time should have passed? How many apologies should he have made, and to whom? What if some of those apologies aren't accepted?

- ▶ Should a spiritual teacher who has transgressed but made amends be permitted to serve in positions of authority in the larger hierarchy of the spiritual tradition? On the governing boards of foundations or nonprofits? What if he hasn't made amends? What if he's made amends, but some people aren't satisfied with them? How much time should pass before any such appointment should be seriously considered?

- ▶ What about a spiritual teacher who has impeccable boundaries within his spiritual community, but has multiple lovers from outside it? Is that okay? Okay with whom? What is the community's right, role, or obligation in such a situation? Is it even the community's business? Who is "the community" in such a case? Its governing body? A consensus of its membership? What if one community leader discovers that the teacher has been in a long and mutually faithful *ménage a trois*?

► If a spiritual teacher transgresses and quickly leaves the community, but reappears a year later and asks for the chance to apologize, make amends, go through a restorative justice process, and rejoin the community as a student, should he be permitted to? What process—and what criteria—should community leaders use to make that decision? Under what circumstances should a teacher be told, "No amends, no restoration, no reconciliation; stay away"?

► If a teacher transgresses as a young man, but soon makes amends and lives a wholesome life thereafter, at what point does his early transgression become irrelevant? When he is forty? Fifty? Sixty? Never?

► Certain types of spiritual teaching—working individually with koans in Zen Buddhism, for example—can *only* be done one-to-one. Should a talented koan teacher who has transgressed be required to teach only via telephone? Should a third person serve as a chaperone in one-to-one meetings? Should the teacher simply be prohibited from one-to-one koan work? All work as a spiritual teacher?

► What about a wonderfully wise, inspiring, and transgression-free teacher whose own teacher regularly transgressed (or continues to transgress today)? How do the actions of the teacher's teacher reflect on them? Should the teacher be required or expected to criticize their own teacher, or urge him to clean up his act? If so, required or expected by whom? What if the teacher refuses to criticize their teacher, and has only words of praise for him? What if the teacher deflects all questions about their own teacher's actions?

These questions are inexhaustible, in both their number and variations. Yet real life presents us regularly with precisely these kinds of questions.

Dilemmas such as these need to be sanely and public discussed. Thus, in late 2010, I started thespiritualteachersite.com and sexandthespiritualteacher.com, which are forums for raising and discussing them. I offer a new question every week or two, and I invite respectful online discussion. I also welcome suggestions for future questions.*

---

* Full disclosure: I also use these sites to promote my books and to let people know of my upcoming travels and talks. But I keep the promotion and online discussions quite separate.

Afterword

Knowledge, Action, and Power

by Anne Katherine

MANY YEARS AGO when I was in graduate school, a well-known guru came to my college to speak to a packed audience. Afterward, I was invited, along with some other doctoral candidates in my psychology department, to a weekend retreat with this spiritual teacher.

Here, in a relaxed lovely setting, we were invited to expand our spiritual horizons, to open ourselves. But the teacher had a different agenda than what I had expected, one that made me increasingly uncomfortable.

The retreat turned into a thinly disguised sexual romp for the guru.

It was the late 1960s, the Summer of Love, and B.B.E. (Before the Boundaries Era). Still, some internal Geiger counter drove me from the private rural setting long before the retreat's official end. At the time, I thought *I* was the one out of step, a prude. It never occurred to me to mention the situation to the department head. I thought it would make me look bad for not being morally flexible.

A similar reticence can affect other victims of exploitive spiritual teachers—not just individuals, but communities that can themselves be victimized when a spiritual teacher exploits his followers.

Scott's words taught me that my 1968 guru was a libertine. And I can testify from personal experience that Scott is correct: that despite their lack of hypocrisy, even a libertine can cause a ripple effect of damage.

Today, the skeletons are out of the closet. We are no longer naïve. We know we have a responsibility to blow whistles and to support unwitting victims of slick operators. But pieces were still missing, and Scott's book gives them to us: a way to discriminate among human weakness, power addiction, and predation. It also provides a language for communities to use in healing themselves. Most importantly, it tells us which transgressors *cannot* be given a second chance—and how to prevent sexual transgression in the first place.

One potency of spiritual practice is the assurance that we are forgiven, redeemed, and given second chances. Surprisingly, this becomes the Achilles' heel of most spiritual communities. In an attempt to follow our spiritual ideal, we feel compelled to extend forgiveness and second chances to others as well, sometimes mindlessly.

Sex and the Spiritual Teacher shows us when we can follow this impulse, and when we must not, for the sake of the innocents in an exploitive teacher's path. This is a boundary we must hold, no matter how open our hearts or how beguiled our thoughts.

Sex and the Spiritual Teacher fills the gap between the knowledge that harm-doing exists and the wherewithal to do something about it—not only after harm has been done, but before it even starts.

With this fresh understanding, I am empowered to bring more wisdom to my own spiritual community and to help create an atmosphere that protects all of us.

I propose that this book be required reading for students of any religious tradition, for any apprentice spiritual teacher or clergyperson, and for the governing bodies of every religious institution.

Let us together hold the boundary that makes spiritual communities safe.

Recommended Resources

On building healthy relationships with spiritual teachers:

▶ *The Nine Stages of Spiritual Apprenticeship: Understanding the Student-Teacher Relationship* by Greg Bogart (Dawn Mountain Press, 1997)

▶ *A Rare and Precious Thing: The Possibilities and Pitfalls of Working with a Spiritual Teacher* by John Kain (Bell Tower, 2006)

▶ thespiritualteachersite.com. This site, which I operate, offers guidance and information on building strong, safe relationships with spiritual teachers.

On spiritual arrogance and misapprehension:

▶ *Halfway Up the Mountain: The Error of Premature Claims to Enlightenment* by Mariana Caplan (Hohm Press, 1999)

▶ *Holy Madness: Spirituality, Crazy-Wise Teachers, and Enlightenment* by Georg Feuerstein (Hohm Press, 2006)

▶ *Prophetic Charisma: The Psychology of Revolutionary Religious Personalities* by Len Oakes (Syracuse University Press, 1997)

On personal boundaries:

- ▶ *Boundaries: Where You End and I Begin* by Anne Katherine (Hazelden, 1994; Fireside, 2000)
- ▶ *Where to Draw the Line: How to Set Healthy Boundaries Every Day* by Anne Katherine (Fireside, 2000)

On spiritual discernment:

- ▶ *Eyes Wide Open: Cultivating Discernment on the Spiritual Path* by Mariana Caplan (Sounds True, 2009)

On sexual misconduct by spiritual teachers, clergy, and other helping professionals:

- ▶ *Understanding Clergy Misconduct in Religious Systems* by Candace R. Benyei (Routledge, 1998)
- ▶ *Stripping the Gurus: Sex, Violence, Abuse and Enlightenment* by Geoffrey D. Falk (Million Monkeys Press, 2009); also available as a free download at strippingthegurus.com
- ▶ *When a Congregation Is Betrayed: Responding to Clergy Misconduct* edited by Beth Ann Gaede (The Alban Institute, 2005)
- ▶ *Restoring the Soul of a Church: Healing Congregations Wounded by Clergy Sexual Misconduct* edited by Nancy Myer Hopkins and Mark Laaser (The Liturgical Press, 1995)
- ▶ *Questions and Answers About Clergy Sexual Misconduct* by Elisabeth A. Horst (The Liturgical Press, 2000)
- ▶ *At Personal Risk: Boundary Violations in Professional-Client Relationships* by Marilyn R. Peterson (Norton, 1992)
- ▶ *Responding to Clergy Misconduct* (FaithTrust Institute, 2009)
- ▶ *Sex in the Forbidden Zone* by Peter Rutter (Ballantine, 1997)

On preventing sexual misconduct by spiritual teachers and leaders:

▶ *Preventing Sexual Abuse in Congregations* by Karen A. McClintock (The Alban Institute, 2004)
▶ *Safe Harbor: Guidelines, Process and Resources for Ethics and Right Conduct in Buddhist Communities* edited by Alan Senauke (Buddhist Peace Fellowship, 2004)

On restorative justice:

▶ *The Spiritual Roots of Restorative Justice* by Michael L. Hadley (State University of New York Press, 2001)
▶ *Restorative Justice: Ideas, Practices, Debate* by Gerry Johnstone (Willan Publishing, 2001)
▶ *Critical Issues in Restorative Justice* edited by Howard Zehr and Barb Toews (Criminal Justice Press, 2004)
▶ *The Little Book of Restorative Justice* by Howard Zehr (Good Books, 2002)

On circles:

▶ *The Little Book of Circle Processes* by Kay Pranis (Good Books, 2005)
▶ *Peacemaking Circles* by Kay Pranis, Barry Stuart, and Mark Wedge (Living Justice Press, 2003)

Organizations and consultants that can help spiritual groups avoid sexual misconduct and/or heal in the wake of it:

▶ Jan and Hogen Bays (zendust.org). Work primarily with spiritual groups in Eastern traditions. Both are Zen priests and teachers who have trained through FaithTrust Institute and the Alban Institute (see below). Jan Chozen Bays is also a

228 Sex and the Spiritual Teacher

pediatrician and the author of several books; Hogen Bays is also a therapist who has treated sex offenders.

▶ Marie Fortune and affiliated consultants, FaithTrust Institute (faithtrustinstitute.org). FaithTrust consultants come from Christian, Muslim, and Jewish backgrounds and work with spiritual groups in all traditions, both Western and Eastern. FaithTrust Institute offers a wide range of services and products that support the spiritual health of religious groups, members, teachers, and leaders. Fortune is a United Church of Christ minister and the author of *Love Does No Harm*, *Is Nothing Sacred?*, *Responding to Clergy Misconduct*, *Sexual Violence: The Sin Revisited*, and *Keeping the Faith: Guidance for Christian Women Facing Abuse*.

▶ Karen A. McClintock (healthycongregation.com). McClintock is a clinical psychologist who works with spiritual groups in all traditions, both Western and Eastern. Her books include *Preventing Sexual Abuse in Congregations*, *Sexual Shame*, and *Healthy Disclosure: Solving Communication Quandaries in Congregations*.

▶ Susan Nienaber, the Alban Institute (alban.org). The Alban Institute is an ecumenical organization that supports spiritual health, healing, and vitality in religious groups. Nienaber is a United Methodist minister, psychotherapist, and mediator whose specialties include professional boundaries, managing conflicts, and trauma recovery. She works with spiritual groups in all traditions, both Western and Eastern.

▶ Yvonne Rand (goats@infoasis.com). Rand is a Zen priest who works with spiritual groups in all traditions.

▶ Gary Schoener (grschoener@walkin.org). Schoener is a psychologist who works with spiritual groups in all traditions.

▶ Alan Senauke (alan@clearviewproject.org). Senauke is a Zen priest who works primarily with Buddhist groups.

Notes

CHAPTER 1

p. 6n   "In multiple studies...96% of helping professionals who had sex with
their clients, patients, or students were male." This is a consensus figure from the book *Sexual Intimacy Between Therapists and Patients*
by Kenneth S. Pope and Jacqueline Bouhoutsos (Praeger, 1986), and
cited by Peter Rutter in his book *Sex in the Forbidden Zone* (Fawcett,
1991), page 22. Pope has written many books and articles—alone and
in collaboration with several other clinicians—on sex between helping
professionals and their clients. Bouhoutsos has also done a good deal
of groundbreaking work on the subject.

p. 9   "...63% of all teachers surveyed had had sex with at least one of
their students." The results of Jack Kornfield's survey were published
in the July/August 1985 issue of *Yoga Journal*, in Kornfield's article
"Sex Lives of the Gurus." Kornfield surveyed fifteen Zen teachers, nine
Hindu and Jain swamis, twenty-four Theravada Buddhist teachers,
and six Tibetan Buddhist teachers.

p. 9n   "Multiple studies show that, in fact, roughly 10–20%...of male professionals in these fields have had sex with the clients, patients, or
students, and that 30% of clergy have been sexual with their congregants." In his book *Sex in the Forbidden Zone* (cited earlier), Peter
Rutter observes, "Studies of sexual contact in universities show, with
great consistency, that 20 percent to 30 percent of female students have
been approached sexually by their professors. A recent report found
that 17 percent of female graduate students in psychology had become
sexually intimate with a professor during their training, and that an
additional 30 percent turned away unwelcome advances" (page 39).
A study in the *American Journal of Psychiatry*, also cited by Rutter
(page 41), revealed that 13% of physicians reported sexual involvement with patients; of these, 80% reported intimate contact with an

average of six patients. In his article "Sexual Exploitation of Patients: How It Begins Before It Happens," which appeared in the February 1989 issue of *Psychiatric Annals*, Robert I. Simon estimates that 15–25% of all types of clinicians may initiate sex with their patients. In her book *Preventing Sexual Abuse in Congregations* (The Alban Institute, 2004), Karen A. McClintock notes, "Across denominations roughly 30 percent of clergy anonymously report having crossed a sexual boundary and engaged in sexual intimacy with someone in their parish" (page 106). These statistics were compiled from several denominational studies by FaithTrust Institute.

p. 9n   "...sexual exploitation of professional relationships is epidemic in our society." This quote appears on page 15 of Peter Rutter's *Sex in the Forbidden Zone*, cited earlier.

p. 19   "Anyone who wanted to come was welcome...." Brad Warner's quote is from an interview I did with him in St. Paul, Minnesota, on November 30, 2009.

CHAPTER 2

p. 28n   "Portnoy's Complaint: A disorder..." The quote from Philip Roth's *Portnoy's Complaint* appears on page 1 of the 1994 Vintage International edition. The quote from Peter Rutter that immediately follows is from his book *Sex in the Forbidden Zone*, cited earlier, page 165.

CHAPTER 3

p. 46   "...certain people may be neurologically predisposed to sexual addiction." Aviel Goodman's discussion of this theme begins on page 158 of his book *Sexual Addiction: An Integrated Approach* (International Universities Press, 1998).

CHAPTER 4

p. 51   "Being in the teacher role is a powerful position, and, like heroin, such power can be addictive. As students, we often...become enablers, co-conspirators." This quote is from John Kain's *A Rare and Precious Thing: The Possibilities and Pitfalls of Working with a Spiritual Teacher* (Bell Tower, 2006), page 245.

CHAPTER 7

p. 65n   "The path of disillusionment is one of the most potent and instructive..." Mariana Caplan's quote is from her article "Where Are We Going?: The Fate and Failings of Contemporary Spirituality," published in the Spring 2001 issue of *ReVision* magazine. Jack Kornfield's quote is from his book *A Path with Heart* (Bantam, 1993), page 268.

CHAPTER 8

p. 71n   Anne Fausto-Sterling's proposition that we humans have five sexes appears in several of her publications; my source is the article "The Five Sexes: Why Male and Female Are Not Enough," which appeared in the March/April 1993 issue of *The Sciences*, pages 20–24. In 1987, in a literature class taught by Leslie Fiedler at the State University of New York at Buffalo, Fiedler offhandedly made the claim that there are seven human sexes. As a student in this class, I challenged this claim, and Fiedler gave a brief explanation similar to Fausto-Sterling's, but in which he recognized two additional (and rare) genital configurations as separate sexes. John Money's estimation that 4% of people are born intersexual is from Fausto-Sterling's article.

p. 73   The 1992 "private wishes" study, "Private Wishes: Gender Similarities and Differences," was conducted by Howard Ehrlichman and Rosalind Eichenstein and published in the May 1992 (vol. 26, nos. 9–10) issue of the journal *Sex Roles*.

p. 74   "In judging someone's suitability as a partner..." Thomas Wright's quote is from a conversation we had in 1991, which Wright confirmed in a May 3, 2010, email. Wright is best known as the author of the books *Raising Children One Day at a Time* and *Will My Child Grow Up Okay?*

p. 75   "I understand the need for a boundary, but there is an incomparable excitement..." Rev. Grant Bennett's quote is from Peter Rutter's book *Sex in the Forbidden Zone*, cited earlier, page 54.

p. 75n   "Some professionals (clergy, physicians, attorneys) will have sex with those entrusted to their care..." Patrick J. Carnes's quote is from his book *The Betrayal Bond* (Health Communications, 1997), page 10.

p. 77   "...profoundly affects physique, behavior, mood, and self-understanding..." Andrew Sullivan's quote is from his article "The He Hormone," published in the April 2, 2000, issue of *The New York Times*. My information on the 1993 study, which showed that men with high testosterone levels are more likely to have failed marriages, is also from this article.

p. 77   "When Stanford researchers injected newborn female rats with testosterone..." This research was reported by Deborah Blum in her book *Sex on the Brain* (Penguin, 1998), page 163.

p. 78   "In 1999, for example, Drew (formerly Susan) Seidman underwent the lengthy process..." Seidman's story, and his quoted remarks, are from the article "A Real Man" by Norah Vincent, which appeared in the November 17, 1999, issue of *The Village Voice*.

p. 78   "I can actually feel its power on an almost daily basis...." and "This, then, is what it comes down to..." Both of Andrew Sullivan's quotes are from "The He Hormone," cited earlier.

CHAPTER 9

p. 83n   "...I should drop everything and come study with him..." Alan Lew's quote is from his book *One God Clapping* (Jewish Lights, 2001), page 55.

p. 85   "...using spiritual ideas and practices to sidestep personal, emotional 'unfinished business'..." John Welwood's quote is from his book *Toward a Psychology of Awakening* (Shambhala, 2002), page 207. Robert Masters has also published a book on this topic, called *Spiritual Bypassing* (North Atlantic Books, 2010).

CHAPTER 10

p. 89   "Success itself puts a man at higher risk for feeling that he can make his own rules..." Peter Rutter's quote is from his book *Sex in the Forbidden Zone*, cited earlier, page 166.

CHAPTER 11

p. 91   "Any time people are following you, you've got alpha status." John Alexander's quote is from his book *How to Become an Alpha Male* (Lulu/John Alexander Enterprises, 2005), page 67.

p. 92   "Wherever they are and whatever they do, they stand out from the crowd . . ." Kate Luderman and Eddie Erlandson's quotes are from their book *Alpha Male Syndrome* (Harvard Business School Press, 2006), pages 1 and 3. John Alexander's quote is from page 46 of *How to Become an Alpha Male*, cited earlier.

p. 93   "When alpha personalities 'are at their worst, they go down in flames...'" Luderman and Erlandson's quotes are from pages 8 and 13 of their book *Alpha Male Syndrome*, cited earlier. The four types of alphas noted in the following paragraph are summarized on pages 43–45 of that book. On page ix, Luderman and Erlandson also reflect on the subject of men being raised to believe they have special talents, promise, or karma.

CHAPTER 12

p. 98   "However, psychologist Karen McClintock...estimates that 65–75% of clergy (of both sexes) receive such advances." This estimate is from McClintock's book *Preventing Sexual Abuse on Congregations*, cited earlier, page 70.

CHAPTER 13

p. 102   "[T]here is spiritual growth, and there is psychological development..." Mariana Caplan's quote is from an interview with David Ian Miller in SFGate.com, published on March 9, 2009, and accessible at http://articles.sfgate.com/2009–03–09/living/17118302_1_unconditional-love-spiritual-jake.

CHAPTER 19

p. 128   "Tantra provides powerful methods for getting in touch with our essential wholeness..." Lama Thubten Yeshe's quote is from his book *Introduction to Tantra: The Transformation of Desire*, Revised Edition (Wisdom Publications, 2001), page 19.

p. 130   "...Tantra in our industrial societies is often an ersatz version..." Daniel Odier's quote is from his book *Desire: The Tantric Path of Awakening* (Inner Traditions, 2001), page 132.

p. 130   Here are the pitches for pseudo-tantric teachings, matched with their sources: "...the ecstatically pleasurable power of Tantric love" (sourcetantra.com); "the best sex ever" (*The Complete Idiot's Guide to Tantric Sex* by Dr. Judy Kurlansky [Alpha, 2001], page 1); "sexual education, enhancement, healing, and advice" (thepleasureparadigm.com).

CHAPTER 20

p. 139   "You have to use the same moral standards for an enlightened person as you do for a normal person...." Sangye Drolma's quote is from Greg Bogart's book *The Nine Stages of Spiritual Apprenticeship: Understanding the Student-Teacher Relationship* (Dawn Mountain Press, 1997), page 203.

p. 139   "Some might say that the higher degree of enlightenment..." Norman Fischer's quote is from "Sex, Lies, and Buddhism," which appeared in the Summer 2010 issue of *Buddhadharma*, page 60.

CHAPTER 21

p. 141 "If a relationship has to be secret, you shouldn't be in it." Regina Brett's quote is from her May 28, 2006, column in the *Cleveland Plain Dealer*, "Regina Brett's 45 Life Lessons and 5 to Grow On."

CHAPTER 22

p. 147 "But there are also some good reasons spiritual teachers seem to end up in the sack with their students so often..." Brad Warner's quote is from his book *Zen Wrapped in Karma Dipped in Chocolate* (New World Library, 2009), page 218.

CHAPTER 23

p. 156 "A crisis can have the effect of breaking open a congregation..." Nancy Myer Hopkins' quote is from her book *The Congregational Response to Clergy Betrayals of Trust* (The Liturgical Press, 1998), page 49.

CHAPTER 24

p. 159 "The problems of teachers cannot easily be separated from the communities around them..." Jack Kornfield's quote is from his book *A Path with Heart*, cited earlier, page 255.

p. 162 "...we should never underestimate the power of the explicit acknowledgment of violation in the process of healing ..." Marie Fortune's quote is from her book *Is Nothing Sacred?* (Wipf & Stock, 2008), page 115.

CHAPTER 27

p. 177 "No one trusted the hierarchical structure of the community..." Michael Downing's quote is from his book *Shoes Outside the Door: Desire, Devotion, and Excess at San Francisco Zen Center* (Counterpoint, 2002), page 325.

p. 178 The story of Kripalu's rise, implosion, reconfiguration, and renewal is widely told, and Kripalu's leaders are quite open about it. An honest and detailed account can be accessed at kripalu.org/about_us/491/.

CHAPTER 29

p. 190 "Teachers who don't regularly sit in the student seat are likely to run into issues of abuse of power or boundary violations." Yvonne Rand's quote is from a phone interview I did with her on April 30, 2010.

CHAPTER 31

p. 202   "[T]he power of family rules within the system..." Candace R. Benyei's quote is from her book *Understanding Clergy Misconduct in Religious Systems* (Routledge, 1998), page 149.

p. 205   Marie Fortune's elements of healing for a wounded spiritual community appear in multiple publications, including Fortune's book *Is Nothing Sacred?*, cited earlier, page 113, and the web page pcusa.org/sexualmisconduct/rebuilding-trust.htm.

Acknowledgments

THIS BOOK BEGAN in 1999, when Alice Erickson, the longtime administrative director of the Minnesota Zen Center, left MZC and began working as my assistant. It was her idea to write a book on the subject, and I strongly encouraged her to do so. As the years passed, however, Alice's interest in the project waned—but mine grew. She was very happy to pass the baton. Thanks, Alice, for getting me started.

Thanks, too, to Dharma Field Zen Center. In 2004 I gave a student talk called "Sex and the Sangha" at Dharma Field; some pieces of this talk became themes of this book.

I'm grateful to everyone who read this book in manuscript or outline form and made helpful suggestions for strengthening it. Special thanks to Jan Chozen Bays, who, in multiple conversations and emails, helped me clarify and highlight some essential points— and then, once the book was finished, read it yet again and offered further useful comments. I also offer my thanks to Roger Jackson of Carleton College, who read a draft of my chapter on tantra and provided important suggestions and corrections. Thanks also to Kiera Van Gelder and Mic Hunter for their assistance with some descriptions and terms.

My further thanks to Mic Hunter for writing the introduction, and to Anne Katherine for writing the afterword—but, even more, for all the good work they've done (and continue to do) to reduce sexual exploitation and keep folks safe.

I'm deeply grateful to the many writers whose nonfiction books have taught me so much by example. I bow especially deeply to Bruce Bawer, Ellis Cose, Mariana Caplan, Barbara Ehrenreich, Tom Friedman, Paul Fussell, Malcolm Gladwell, Chip and Dan Heath, Anne Katherine, Jonah Lehrer, P.J. O'Rourke, Michael Pollan, Neil Postman, Thomas Sowell, and Deborah Tannen. In reviewing this list, I am reminded yet again that brilliant writing adheres to no ideology or segment of the sociopolitical spectrum.

Two of the most important things I learned about writing a book, however, come from a couple of my own spiritual teachers, Steve Hagen and Tim McCarthy. I'll paraphrase both teachers' advice here. From Steve: "Sooner or later, you have to stop reading and researching, and just say what you have to say." From Tim: "Write what you need to write. Worry about support, sources, and citations later. But if wise sources don't support what you say, consider saying something different." My client Terry O'Neill gave me this equally valuable advice: "Start out by asking yourself, 'What am I trying to achieve?' Then use your answer to this question to guide you as you make each decision." My thanks to all three of you; without these pieces of secular wisdom, I might never have finished this book.

Many thanks to my agent, Barbara Moulton, who worked long and hard to find the right publisher for this book—and who found its best possible home at Wisdom Publications.

My great thanks to Josh Bartok, my editor at Wisdom, who immediately saw the importance of this book and the need for it. To my knowledge, Josh is the only person in North America who is both an editor of consumer books and a spiritual teacher. That alone would have made him the ideal editor for this book. But he turned out to be a pleasure to work with, and he made many wise suggestions that resulted in a considerably better book.

Thanks also to Joe Evans and Caroline DeVane at Wisdom, for their energetic publicity work.

Thanks to all my past and present spiritual teachers, in all their wisdom and with all their warts.

My widespread thanks to everyone who reads this book, takes

it to heart, and helps to create spiritual communities and teacher-student relationships that are safer and more spiritually intimate.

My most heartfelt thanks of all go to my wife Ariella, whose support for this project never wavered for an instant.

Index

secrecy
 exploiters and, 141–42
 and sexual misconduct, community
  response to, 161–64
 student-teacher romance and,
  150–51
seduction
 accusations of, 8
 libertine teachers and, 114–16
 students' seduction of spiritual
  teachers, 62, 97–100, 216
 teachers' seduction of students, 6,
  37
Seidman, Drew, 78
Senauke, Alan, 227, 228
serial errants, 27
serial exceptionalists, 27
sex as spiritual teaching or tool,
  35–36, 121–26
sexiness of spiritual teachers, 12,
  59–62, 93
sexiness of students, 12, 97–100
sexual addiction, 46–47
sexual assault, 35
sexual deal-making, 37
sexual guidelines and expectations,
  183–85
sexual misconduct between clinicians
 and clients, 2, 9, 229n9
sexual misconduct of spiritual
 teachers
 causes of, 7–10
 confessions of, 141–42
 ethical concerns about, 30–31
 excuses and justifications for, 38–39
 forced celibacy and, 111
 guidelines and procedures for dealing with, 172, 183–84
 vs. misconduct of ordinary clergy,
  15–17

prevalence of, 8–10
 questions about, 220–22
 reinstatement of teachers after,
  212–14
 resources for understanding and
  preventing, 226–27
 responses of healthy spiritual communities, 201–14
 safety and job fit, 31–32
 secrecy, privacy, and disclosure,
  161–64
 tradition of, 6–8
 why it matters, 13–15
sexual release, options for, 95
sexual role models, 56–57
Shedd Aquarium, 219
Simon, Robert I., 229–30n9
Solomon, 134
spiritual authority vs. organizational
 authority, 166–68
spiritual communities
 consultants for, 201–4
 contacts outside of, importance of,
  102
 definition, as used in this book, ix
 disillusionment of, 102, 143–44
 disillusionment vs. dissolution of,
  153–56
 dissolution of, 212
 guidelines, codes, and policies,
  169–73
 healing of, 201–14
 healthy communities, description
  of, 159–60, 175–77
 Kripalu Center for Yoga and
  Health, 91–92, 178–79, 212
 organizational principles for,
  165–68
 pseudo-tantric teachers and, 131

About the Author

PHOTO BY ARIELLA TILSEN

Since 1978, SCOTT EDELSTEIN has studied happily and productively with several spiritual teachers, including Tim McCarthy, Dainin Katagiri, Toni Packer, and (currently) Steve Hagen. As the friend of many spiritual teachers from a variety of traditions, he has also spent much time with them "off duty," sometimes serving as confidant. He is a longtime practitioner of both Buddhism and Judaism, and a committed proponent of serious spirituality in all forms and traditions. He has been a member of Methodist, Quaker, Buddhist, and Jewish congregations.

Scott's short work on spiritual topics has appeared in *Shambhala Sun*, *American Jewish World*, *The Writer*, the anthology *What About God?* (Upper Room Books), and elsewhere. His book *Breathe, Listen, Learn: A Practical Guide for Everyone Who Wants (or Has) a Spiritual Teacher*, will be published in 2012 by Wisdom Publications. Scott is the author of fifteen other books on a wide range of subjects, including writing and publishing, success in college, and recovery from addiction.

About Mic Hunter

MIC HUNTER is a marriage and family therapist whose books include the bestseller *Abused Boys: The Neglected Victims of Sexual Abuse*. Mic is also the author of many other books, including *Joyous Sexuality: Healing from the Effects of Family Sexual Dysfunction* and *Honor Betrayed: Sexual Abuse in America's Military*. In 2007, malesurvivor.org established the Mic Hunter award for leadership in the field of sexual abuse prevention at City University of New York's John Jay College of Criminal Justice.

About Anne Katherine

ANNE KATHERINE is the author of the bestselling *Boundaries: Where You End and I Begin*, *Where to Draw the Line: How to Set Healthy Boundaries Every Day*, and several other books. Now retired, for many years she was a psychologist in private practice, working with clients on issues of personal boundaries, sexual abuse, and spiritual growth.

About Wisdom Publications

To LEARN MORE about Wisdom Publications, a nonprofit publisher, and to browse our other books dedicated to skillful living, visit our website at www.wisdompubs.org.

You may request a copy of our catalog online or by writing to this address:

Wisdom Publications
199 Elm Street
Somerville, Massachusetts 02144 USA
Telephone: 617-776-7416
Fax: 617-776-7841
Email: info@wisdompubs.org
www.wisdompubs.org

Wisdom is a nonprofit, charitable 501(c)(3) organization affiliated with the Foundation for the Preservation of the Mahayana Tradition (FPMT).